Your First Year in Real Estate

Available from
YOUR FIRST YEAR Series:

Your First Year As an Elementary School Teacher
Your First Year As a High School Teacher
Your First Year As a Nurse
Your First Year in Real Estate
Your First Year in Sales

Your First Year in

Real Estate

Making the Transition from Total
Novice to Successful Professional

D I R K Z E L L E R

 T H R E E R I V E R S P R E S S
N E W Y O R K

Published by Three Rivers Press, New York, New York.
Member of the Crown Publishing Group, a division of Random House, Inc., New York.
www.randomhouse.com

THREE RIVERS PRESS and the Tugboat design are registered trademarks of Random House, Inc.

Originally published by Prima Publishing, Roseville, California, in 2001.

All products mentioned in this book are trademarks of their respective companies.

Printed in the United States of America

Library of Congress Cataloging-in-Publication Data

Zeller, Dirk.
    Your first year in real estate : making the transition from total novice to successful professional / Dirk Zeller.
        p. cm. — (Your first year)
    Includes index.
    1. Real estate business—Vocational guidance. 2. Real estate business. I. Title. II. Your first year series.

HD1375.Z45   2001
333.33'023'73 — dc21
                                                                        2001021657

ISBN 0-7615-3412-1

10 9 8 7 6

First Edition

To all our Real Estate Champion coaching clients, who have implemented many of the techniques, skills, and tools contained within this book and have transformed their businesses and lives. I am grateful for the honor of having a front row seat in your lives. There is no greater joy for me in life than to watch the results you all are achieving.

Contents

Acknowledgments ───────────────────────────

There are so many people who have impacted my life that it would be impossible to thank them all. Each of us receives the blessings that people pour into our lives. In my 39 years I have been blessed beyond measure.

Certainly, the most important of all is my wife, Joan, without whose constant encouragement and support my real estate career would not have reached the heights that it has. Without her, this book you are reading also would not exist. Her advice and wise counsel throughout my real estate career and now, in my speaking, writing, and coaching career, has been truly heaven-sent. She has been instrumental in the building of Real Estate Champions.

To the team at Real Estate Champions. No one could ask for better people to work with. In building a company you need to surround yourself with the best. From the coaches to the administrative staff we have done that.

Special thanks must be given to Abbott Lawrence, the president of Real Estate Champions. Thank you for many years of guidance and wise counsel. Also, for your careful eye when editing and proofreading my work. You have been blessing me with your insight for most of my life. A better friend no one could find.

To Julie Porfirio, the rock at Real Estate Champions. Your endless hours compiling, typing, and creating produced this end result. Without your organizational skills we would not have the global impact for the real estate community that we do.

Lastly, to my parents, Norm and Becky Zeller. What an honor to be your son. You both have taught me so much. Without your gifts of hard work, passion for learning, persistence, and commitment, I would not be fulfilling my true purpose in life. Thank you for going the extra mile as parents to instill them in me, when it would have been easier not too.

Introduction _____

The real estate field is one of the most exciting career choices you can consider. Millions of people have considered entering the real estate field, comparing themselves and their abilities to real estate agents they know. Family members and friends tell them, "You should sell real estate!" They often view what Realtors do as easy money. You may be thinking the same thing most people do about Realtors. My first response to those thoughts is that what you perceive from the outside looking in may not be the whole truth about the profession. What many people deem to be easy can often be truly difficult when viewed up close.

According to the National Association of Realtors, the median income for all Realtors is $43,500. The median income for brokers or broker associates is $63,100. This clearly shows that the more educated you are in real estate skills and techniques, the more income that you make. Your goal should be to educate yourself regularly so you can increase your income. The National Association of Realtors is the largest professional association, representing nearly 730,000 members involved in all aspects of the real estate industry. They are regularly evaluating the profile of their members in demographic, economic, and professional characteristics. As a new agent, you must be prepared to work hard and diligently to achieve success.

My desire is not to paint a bleak picture, just an accurate one. The truth is that with the right steps, desire, and determination, you can earn two, three, or even four times the median income in your first year. I have one absolute belief. That belief is, "If I can do it, so can you." My journey into real estate started in the summer of 1990 when I had just moved back to Portland, Oregon. I had closed my event promotion business in Denver and was searching for my next career.

I was truly at a crossroads in my professional life. I was 28 years old and had little to show for the six years I had worked after college. The selection of my career was of paramount importance this time.

My desire for a career that enabled me to control the income, the time invested and, ultimately, the outcome was enormous. I truly wanted the fruits of my labors to be immense. I wanted the reward for my hard work to come to me, not someone else. Maybe you are feeling that way right now.

I was frustrated and discouraged that my last six years of work had not produced more wealth. This was not how I had imagined myself at 28 years old. People often enter real estate sales from similar circumstances. They try many other job options and careers and finally find their way into real estate sales. They blossom in the flexibility of hours. They embrace the opportunity to earn any amount of money they desire. They want to build a business that allows them to continually increase their income by 20 percent, 30 percent, or even 50 percent annually. Those were all the things I wanted as well.

There is nothing more exciting than starting a new venture. The new venture of real estate sales unfolded in December of 1990. I recall that I struggled starting out as most agents do. You, like me, will have that lost feeling many times early in your career, the "Why am I doing this? Is it really worth it?" feeling. Those feelings can be compounded when the income doesn't come as fast as the bills and when there is a lot of month at the end of the money.

One of the challenges in real estate is learning to budget your money. Especially early in one's career there can be a long span of time between commission checks. You have to avoid the temptation to spend it all. To hold some of the money back in savings is a skill that needs to be learned.

For many people it will also be the first time they are responsible for their own taxes. For years we work as an employee and now we are entering the independent contractor world in real estate. We must learn to save a portion of each commission check to pay the taxes on the earnings. I, like most agents, learned that lesson the hard way. My first year in the business I didn't save the money for my taxes. When tax time came around I needed to sell a few houses just to pay the tax bill. Fortunately I had to be taught that lesson only once. There are many agents who replay that song year after year after year.

One of the principles that I have learned in the last eleven years since that start in December of 1990 is this: Success comes to those who are willing to persist a little longer. When you have those feelings of frustration and discouragement in your career, you will have to choose to control them or they will eventually control you.

In the end we all have those feelings. It's what actions we take that matter most when we have those feelings. I had those feelings all the time early in my career. I used those feelings to fuel the fire of personal development. If I had not gotten hooked on the books and audiocassette tapes that changed my life, I would not have had the career in real estate sales that I did. You obviously have the same desire that I had in my early career or you would not be reading this book. The quest for personal expansion of knowledge and skill lasts a lifetime. We should never stop learning.

There is a story that I share from the platform. It's commencement day at a large university. Two students who are set to graduate later that day are walking through the commons rather excited about the day's activities. One student says to the other, "I am so excited to graduate today. I am so tired of studying and reading that I won't read another book for as long as I live." They both agree and laugh and keep walking. What they don't know is the president of the university is walking behind them and he hears this exchange between the graduating seniors. The university president was disappointed that these two graduates didn't understand the value of an education while at his institution. The university and faculty didn't fire up their furnaces of learning while they were there.

In the end these students didn't even understand the word *commencement*. They were going through a commencement exercise later in the day without the true knowledge of what it was about. The word commencement means the beginning. They were at the beginning of their educational lives, not the end. They were at the point when the studying and the books they read from that point forward would have the biggest impact on how their lives turned out. Yet, they missed one of the key elements of the university experience, which is to acquire the desire to be a lifelong learner.

My friend, Jim Rohn, describes it best. "Your formal education will make you a living, your personal education will make you a fortune." Jim is a brilliant man and absolutely right. Once I learned and applied this quote of Jim's, my life was transformed.

At the time I entered real estate sales in late 1990, I could count on less than one hand the number of books I had read in the six years since I left Willamette University without graduating. I could count on less than one hand the number of seminars that I had attended. The worst number I could also count on one hand was what I had in my savings account and checking account. I was to find out later there was a direct correlation between all those numbers. The truth is they are linked both positively and negatively.

Since that point I cannot count the number of books that I have read or the number of seminars that I have attended. I don't know how many tape series I own or how many times I have listened to each one. In all these categories of learning the numbers are too high to count. My income and savings have dramatically increased as well. I do not say this to brag but to encourage. I truly believe if I can achieve what I have achieved, you can also. God gave us all tremendous gifts; our job is learning to apply and utilize them, to expand our influence and wealth for our families, our communities, and the world.

Selecting the Right Company

Welcome to your new career in real estate! You have chosen what is for many people a very challenging and rewarding labor of love: selling real estate. The fact that you are here, reading this book, is a good sign: You are already looking for an edge, advantages, and knowledge that will help push you to the top of your profession. So let's begin.

First Things First

It's very easy to get swept away in the emotion and excitement of your new career, to see dollar signs in your eyes without thoroughly researching the facts. Although it is important to dive into your career headfirst, it is also essential to make sure both of your eyes are wide open. You need to research, learn, and prepare for your new profession because, ultimately, the company that you select to first "hang your license" with can make or break your start and your career in this business. In other words, you must begin your new career *before* you get your license.

Licensing Training Programs

Many real estate companies offer licensing training programs. These programs will help you prepare for and pass your state and national licensing exams. Some of these firms teach you through classroom programs aimed at meeting the minimum requirements in your state, and often these classroom programs are augmented with tapes, workbooks, and other materials that you can study outside of the classroom.

In addition, many firms offer their own pre-licensing programs at no cost to you; others will charge you a few dollars to attend. There are some that will pay for these programs and even the cost of the state and national exams. These firms usually will deduct these fees from your first commission check. If you are comfortable with a couple of offices, you might consider the one that is willing to invest in your career financially. Seeking out the best firm for you and talking with them will also help you begin networking within the real estate industry.

Selecting the Right Company for You

Choosing a job for yourself is easy, right? Find a company that is hiring, offer your services, agree on money, and it's all done. If it were only that easy.

Truth is, there are scores of questions you need to ask both the firm and yourself. You must discover what the company can do for you, as well as how you will benefit the company. The situation should be mutually beneficial to you and your office. So what should you look for when searching for the best company for you?

What Every Good Real Estate Company Has

When you sign on with a company, you become an extension of that organization. Before you ever meet a client, he will already have an opinion of your company, and that opinion will influence what your client thinks of you. Learning how to identify a company with a solid history and positive standing in the community is essential to cultivating business and developing your career. A good real estate company, one that will provide you with the resources to succeed, will have several qualities.

A Solid Reputation Is Essential

The reputation of the company is critical. Remember, you are an extension of the company you work for. Until you are able to build a clientele and a following of your own, you will be relying solely on the company's reputation. A buyer or seller will have a positive or negative impression of your company based on its reputation before you ever work with her. That reputation will be based on the success of the company, such as the market share it has achieved and the number of homes it lists and sells annually. The company's involvement with the community is also important.

> *Until you are able to build a clientele and a following of your own, you will be relying solely on the company's reputation.*

A Passion About Customer Service Is a Must

A company's customer service model and service reputation are also important factors. Real estate sales is a service-oriented business

The company you select to work with must share your passion for customer service and must be committed to helping you achieve the level of customer service required to be successful.

where one is paid for results. To be successful, real estate agents must be customer-focused while carefully monitoring time and revenue invested to complete the job. First, you must be committed to providing outstanding customer service. Second, the company you select to work with must share your passion for customer service and must be committed to helping you achieve the level of customer service required to be successful. How you treat your clients, past and present, has a direct bearing on getting listing contracts from a seller and getting that home sold and closed, which is every agent's desired result. Similarly, your ability to secure your representation of the buyer, find him a home, and close the deal is dependent on your level of customer service.

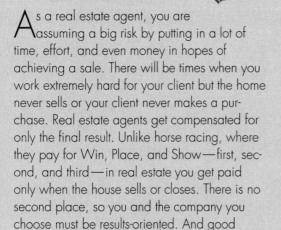

There Is No Second Place

As a real estate agent, you are assuming a big risk by putting in a lot of time, effort, and even money in hopes of achieving a sale. There will be times when you work extremely hard for your client but the home never sells or your client never makes a purchase. Real estate agents get compensated for only the final result. Unlike horse racing, where they pay for Win, Place, and Show—first, second, and third—in real estate you get paid only when the house sells or closes. There is no second place, so you and the company you choose must be results-oriented. And good results are a product of good customer service.

Strong Listing Companies Help a New Agent

Make sure any companies you are considering are strong listing companies. Working for a strong listing company ensures you will have an opportunity to work with a lot of buyers. Most new agents work with more buyers than sellers. Buyers are easier to attract and create relationships with. They are not entrusting their largest asset, their home, to a new agent.

A listing is a contract with a seller to exclusively represent her in selling a home. If an agent acquires a listing, prices the home appropriately, and sells the house, then the agent will get paid. A strong listing office can dramatically help an agent early in her career. When agents and offices have an abundance of listings, they also receive a high volume of ad calls and sign calls. The ad and sign calls lead to buyers and often sellers.

The most successful and productive agents are the agents who focus on listing property, for a regular diet of new listings is the engine that drives the train.

There is an old saying in real estate: "You list, you last." The most successful and productive agents are the agents who focus on listing property, for a regular diet of new listings is the engine that drives the train. To be truly financially successful in real estate sales without having to work all hours of the day and night and on weekends, becoming a strong listing agent is imperative. Aligning with a company that has a large inventory of homes for sale will dramatically help you create success early in your career.

Researching a Company

Once you have determined that a company has a solid reputation, has an effective customer service model, and is a strong listing company, you must research the company and find out the answers to some important questions. The right answers will help you know whether a company is right for you, while the wrong answers will help steer you away to search for a better match.

Seek Out Market Share Information

First, you should inquire about market statistics. Find out the company's market share, how many listings it takes in a year, how many listings sell, how many fail to sell, and how many sales it actually makes. These are numbers, statistics, and statistics don't lie. This information will give you the bottom line about a company and will reflect on its customer service, position in the market, and potential for success on your part.

Check with the Local Board of Realtors

You will want to research the company at your local Board of Realtors. The local board may have market share and other statistics for the company you are interviewing. It is critically important that you check with a third-party resource and verify the statistics that a company provides. Authenticate the figures and make sure the numbers all add up.

The Multiple Listing Service

Another source for market share and statistics is the multiple listing service. In most marketplaces around the country, real estate companies and agents use a multiple listing service to increase exposure. This allows all agents in the Board of Realtors to access every house and property for sale and allows them to sell it. This service is often a separate entity from the Board of Realtors, and it is an invaluable source of

Who's Number One?

There are many companies in real estate who have claimed in recent years to be number one. Some claim to be the biggest real estate companies, in terms of sales, in the world. They have national advertising campaigns staking claim to being number one. Others claim to be number one in service. No wonder the consumer is confused as to whom to believe and do business with! If the industry can't decide who's number one, how can anyone else? Most likely there are statistics and documentation to back each company's claims—it all depends on how you count the numbers. But the bottom line is: Be sure to validate the information you receive from the companies you interview.

information regarding listings and sales of homes. They will help you interpret the truth on the sales in your local area and who controls the market.

Local Business Journals

Lastly, if you live in a major metropolitan area, you may find that the local business journal provides valuable information. Look for special editions that deal with real estate in the marketplace. The journal will often rank bro-

Lots of Agents, Little Production

One word of caution with regard to market share: The number of agents a company has can dramatically affect market share. Many companies have a lot of agents, but each individual agent does little in production. That type of company will not have the personnel who can help you improve your skills much beyond the beginner stage. Make sure you select a company that also allows you to grow and thrive.

kers in size and scope of services. This is another wonderful resource to ensure that you are obtaining the whole truth and starting your career with the right company.

Take a Drive

Another useful research activity is to drive around the community you want to work in and check out the signs. Whose signs are in front of the houses you would want to represent? How many signs are there?

Take the time to drive to the actual office you are considering. Is it in a location that would be effective for business? For some offices it is difficult to see that they are even there. Look at the office from the buyer's or seller's viewpoint. Would you stop there to inquire about their services? When you walk in the door, does the office have the look and feel of a successful business, or does it look and feel chaotic? Some of your future clients will make their decisions on just such an impression.

For a new agent these questions are critical; when you gain experience and skill, the location and amenities are not as important. At that point you will have clients and the skill to create clients and you can generate new business from any location. For now, the look and feel of your office is what your client's impression will be based on.

Got Advertising?

Be sure to research a company's advertising philosophy. For a new agent, the company's frequency and volume of advertising can help you, as a new agent, generate new clients. There are many companies that do very little advertising and rely on the agents themselves to advertise their properties. These companies have a much higher percentage of experienced agents than new agents. Compare advertising over a two-week period. This will give you a good comparison because some companies do bigger ads less frequently, while others engage in lower-profile advertising more frequently.

Display Ads

Note whether the company does display ads or just classifieds. Display ads usually have the company's banner or heading and they gather in one place all the homes the company is advertising. Classifieds are smaller ads arranged by location of the homes. The display ads will give a more impressive appearance to the consumer than spread-out classified ads. A display ad is more elaborate, since a company will often feature an agent or all their agents. Take the time to look at their ads and see how they promote the agents and the company. Is that the image you want to project? Can you see yourself in the ad with the other agents?

Real Estate Book Publications

Another advertising area to review is the real estate book publications you see at the local grocery store. These publications are very effective in marketing and advertising property. They provide a longer shelf life than local newspaper advertisement and offer pictures of the properties. In most markets there are a couple of different magazines to choose from, of varying quality. Does your prospective company present the type of image in these publications that you desire? Are they even present in these advertising mediums? Many companies you will be interviewing may produce their own publication of this nature.

Evaluate the quality, size, and scope of the advertising in these publications. Are there company-sponsored pages with numerous agents on a page, or are there pages for individual agents? When an agent is the only agent on the page, generally the agent has paid for it. You want to make sure that the companies you are considering have spaces for new agents like yourself to use.

You Will Be Courted

Most of your research and investigation should be done *before* you ever sit down for an interview with a broker or manager of a company. One of the objectives of brokers is to recruit new agents. Every day they are out "selling" new agents on their company. Most are prepared and have a solid presentation to convince you their company is the best. And if they are truly wise, they will elicit the help of some of their agents to recruit you. Now, who wouldn't get excited about a company that has a great presentation and parades a couple of agents who make, say, $100,000 a year?

Remember, it's very easy to get wrapped up in excitement, emotion, and enthusiasm. A great salesperson will be able to create those emotions in the buyer. As you seek a company, you are in the buyer role. You are going to be buying a company; its training, and its reputation. Make sure you are purchasing the right vehicle for your career. The broker or manager's job is to create that excitement, emotion, and enthusiasm while showing you the company has the systems and tools for your success. Always remember: Enthusiasm is to selling what yeast is to bread—it makes the dough rise.

The Interview: How to Win the Company Over

After you have done your research on the community; checked out the multiple listing service, the Board of Realtors, and the company's advertising; driven around the neighborhoods; and visited the office, you are ready for the interview! An interview is a chance for you to continue your research into the company, an opportunity for the company to learn how you can benefit it, and the ultimate setting for you to sell your qualities as a potential real estate professional.

What You Need Going into the Interview

The more prepared you are and the better you feel about your appearance and preparation, the smoother the interview will go. Guaranteed. Remember, an interview is an opportunity. Take full advantage of it. Be prepared with a resume, a sharp appearance, and questions and answers.

Prepare a Killer Resume

For the interview you must have a resume. The resume should be short and to the point; one page is best. The broker or manager is going to weigh your attitude, desire, and appearance much heavier than your experience—she can always teach someone with these qualities to be a good salesperson. If you are struggling with your resume, your local public library and bookstores have many books that can help you with that challenge.

Look Good, Feel Good

You have only one opportunity to make a first impression. For an interview, professional attire is a must. Real estate agents pride themselves on being some of the best-dressed professionals in the world. If you go to a real estate seminar or convention, you will think all the attendees make a million dollars a year because they dress like it. Make sure to look the part of a successful person. You want the broker or manager to be able to envision you as a successful real estate agent for his company.

> *Make sure to look the part of a successful person. You want the broker or manager to be able to envision you as a successful real estate agent for his company.*

Whether you are a man or a woman, proper dress is a suit. A conservative suit in navy or black is ideal. There have been numerous studies about the power and authority that is conveyed by a well-dressed man or woman in a navy suit and a white shirt. For years, IBM had a saying that you could wear any color suit and shirt you wanted as long as the suit was blue and the shirt was white. They believed in creating a powerful presence. Your appearance *will* play a part in the outcome of your interview. That may not seem fair, but it is reality. Dress for success!

So You Want to Be a Real Estate Agent

People want to become a real estate agent for many reasons, some good, some bad. I will share my reasons with you: I wanted to make a mid–six figure income and achieve financial independence at an early age. I wanted my income to be tied directly to my effort. I did not want a cap on my earning potential. I was clearly motivated by money. What motivates you? Is it money, serving others, helping people, flexible work hours, controlling your destiny? These are all valid reasons for becoming a real estate agent. It's imperative that you know your reasons before you enter the door for the interview!

Prepare Answers to the Broker's Questions

Before your first interview, prepare to answer a number of questions about why you want to become a real estate agent. Many people go into real estate as a last resort or because they lost their job or think they can make a lot of money easily. The broker wants to find out what your reasons are.

There is no one right reason for wanting to become a real estate agent. The key is to figure out why *you* want to be a one and prepare to explain to your interviewer why this is a good reason and how it will benefit the company. If your explanation is solid and clearly the result of a positive and aggressive attitude, you have just taken a major step toward getting the job you desire.

In addition, you must also prepare for other questions the interviewer may throw your way, including:

- Have you ever been in sales? (Even selling Girl Scout cookies is sales.)
- How do you expect to generate business?
- Are you focused on helping people? Why?
- Are you interested in investing in real estate?
- Are you prepared to work hard?

- Do you work better with a team or as an individual out on your own?

These are all questions a good broker will ask if she is looking for your commitment and desire to succeed.

There is one other question you may hear. It's one I use even today on every interview I conduct: "Why should I hire you?" This one question will often turn the strongest people into Jell-O. It is the key question in the sales process, no matter what you are selling. Every prospect or client will be thinking that question as you do your presentation. If your broker asks you this, your answer will reveal if you have the confidence to be successful. If you have the ability to articulate your skills to others easily and effectively, you will achieve success.

Prepare Your Questions for the Broker

You must also be prepared with your own questions for the broker or manager. You are trying to determine the value of the services the company will provide you in the long run and the level of support and training it will provide for you as a new agent. Here are some of the questions you will want to ask:

What is your training program for new agents?

This area is key when comparing companies. Many do not provide the training necessary to set up a new agent for success. Some companies still use the old-school method: "Here's your desk and here's your phone, go get 'em!" This type of focus will not prepare you for the challenge you are about to face.

However, many companies do provide sales training throughout your career. As a new agent you want as much training as possible, as soon as possible. Make sure to pin down the broker or manager on how often and how soon the training classes take place and where they are held, as well as any costs that come with the training.

Often companies will train new agents in contracts and law, but spend very little time in sales skills and time management. In essence, you are going to open your own new business, and the number one reason for failure in new businesses is lack of sales. Whether you are in real estate a year from now or not will depend on your volume of sales, or the lack thereof. The more training you have in sales skills, scripts, dialogues, prospecting, and lead follow-up techniques, the more success you will have. Make sure your new broker has solid training available in the key disciplines of sales.

As a new agent you want as much training as possible, as soon as possible.

How many new agents do you train annually?

This will tell you the level of experience the company has with new agents. Ask about their success rate. How many agents are still there one year later? If they have a high wash-out rate, be careful. Be leery of the company that gives you the "no one else but you, so we can give you our full attention" bit. You don't want to be surrounded by "top gun" agents who offer little in assistance. I believe that going through training with others is a positive experience. You will have some comrades and role-play partners to learn from and grow with through the learning curve.

Ask to speak to some newer agents who have gone through the training program. Talk with an agent who has sold real estate for a year. Spend a few minutes with someone who is only six months in the business. You need to get a clear picture of how prepared for battle you will be after you leave the training program.

What does it cost me to hang my license with you?

Are there any annual or monthly fees that I pay as the agent? Often, real estate board fees are charged or multiple listing service fees are assessed monthly. Multiple listing service fees can also be assessed by the properties you place with the service. These are called input fees. Who pays those fees?

In addition, all real estate companies have errors and omission insurance, often referred to as E&O insurance. This insurance protects the agent and company if an error is made in representation or service that causes harm to the buyer or seller. I have seen E&O insurance charged on an annual basis, monthly basis, or even per transaction basis.

Also find out who pays for business cards, real estate signs, letterhead, thank-you cards, postage, lockboxes, and advertisements. These are just some of the costs you will incur to begin your real estate sales career.

Find out who pays for business cards, real estate signs, letterhead, thank-you cards, postage, lockboxes, and advertisements.

How will you help me generate business?

Some companies will give you houses to hold open and even run an advertisement for you. Ask if they have floor time. Floor time is the rotation of agents to answer phone calls that come from advertisements and signs. How often will you get floor time? What do you need to do before you are eligible for floor time? These are all key questions. As a new agent, you will be better served by going with a company that gives you floor time. It will give you an opportunity to convert prospects into clients.

Do you have regular office meetings?

Your goal is to be around agents who are doing well and to learn from them when you can. Find out how often meetings occur and what they entail. Does the company provide training in the office meeting or is it just a general office meeting? You will learn from any such office meetings, but obviously the more geared they are to teaching and sharing information, the more you will learn.

How available are others for questions? You will have a tremendous amount of questions early on in your career.

Do you have a formal company orientation process?

This will tell you how organized the company is. Orientation will help you understand who does what in the firm, what procedures you need to follow, and where everything you need is located.

When I have a problem or question whom do I go to?

How available are others for questions? You will have a tremendous amount of questions early on in your career. You will need someone who is available to help you make the right choices quickly. Make sure there will often be someone available to help and answer any key questions you will have in a timely fashion.

Where is the new agent's workspace?

There can be vast differences among companies in regard to the workspace they give different agents. Most companies put new agents and lower-producing agents in the "bullpen." The bullpen is a group of cubicles usually at the center of the office. There is less privacy and more interruptions in this work environment. Rarely will a new agent get the private office we all covet. Carefully assess the bullpen area or the area you may be assigned to sit. Can you work in that environment?

What computer software and hardware do you provide for agents to use?

One of the mainstays of all agents' business is their database. It's where they keep everyone they know and have done business with and all of their leads for future business. Since this database is so critical to success, many companies provide a computer and database software for their new agents. For you to build a solid long-term business you must be able to use a computer database well. Money does not grow on trees—it grows in databases.

Will you put an announcement in the paper and pay for announcement cards if I join your firm?

It's imperative that you notify everyone you can think of about your new career. Often the company will assist you in this process. You might even ask how soon they usually do that!

What's the commission split?

This is the final and biggest question. A commission split is how much you receive of the commission on a sale and how much the company keeps. For a new agent a typical commission split will be around 50 percent for the agent and 50 percent for the broker. Now, that may seem like a lot for the company, but remember that it is doing all the training and providing ongoing support and assistance. It is also, in most cases, providing a desk, a phone, and advertising leads through floor time. The company is making a substantial investment in you. It needs to turn a profit or there will be no company for you to work at!

Make sure to ask if there are any other fees associated with commission. There could be a franchise fee in the range of 5 to 6 percent before the commission split is calculated. You could be paying a transaction fee of $150 to $500 to help with your paperwork. Make sure you get an accurate disclosure of all the costs so you can make the best decision.

The Art of Asking Questions

The last thing to remember is that whoever asks the questions controls the interview or sales presentation. The art of asking questions is the key to success in sales. Many people believe that great salespeople are fast-talking or exceptionally skilled at keeping dialogue going. True master salespersons ask questions to achieve the desired result. They are wonderful at probing for needs and values and problems and attaching their solution to those needs, values, and problems.

During the interview, you may be fortunate enough to be sitting across from a broker or manager who is a great salesperson. A skilled broker or manager is going to ask you questions to determine if you are the right match for his company. Your job is to turn the tables and ask questions to learn about his company so you can be better informed to make your decision.

This is your first sale and maybe the most important one in your career. Make sure to invest the time in preparation and in evaluating companies before the interview. Practice and plan your questions well and conduct yourself in the interview as a sales professional by dressing the part and controlling the dialogue with thoughtful and relevant questions.

If you have interviews with multiple companies, and we hope you will, ideally they will occur within the span of a couple of days.

This way you can keep your questions and impressions fresh in your mind and evaluate the different companies while you still remember them well.

Decision Time

After completing the interview process and talking with a few rookie agents in each firm, you are ready to complete your evaluation and make a decision. Always set yourself up to be the one who decides where you are going to work. There are several things you can do to come up with a conclusive decision about a company.

Rank Each Area of Importance

On a scale of 1 to 10, rate the service each company provides new agents in these key areas:

- training
- office environment
- other agents
- broker/manager
- advertising
- reputation
- market share

Weight Your Decision in Favor of Training

Each of these is a key category, with a bit of extra weight on the training area. For a new agent, training can often make the difference between success and failure. I would even go so far as to recommend selecting a company that might have deficiencies in other categories, but is head and shoulders above the others in training. A good training program for new agents is more than just contracts—it must be focused on prospecting, quality, lead follow-up, the sellers' listing presentation, the buyers' interview, objection handling, and closing techniques. These are the skills of an outstanding salesperson.

Consider Ongoing Training

Be careful to evaluate not only the training a new agent receives, but also the ongoing training the company provides. Are there opportunities for classes, workshops, or even coaching that allow you to continually improve your skills? What form does this training come in? Is it in seminars only? Does the company offer workshops where you'll have time to practice and rehearse what you are learning? Is there a role-playing time for new agents and maybe even role-play partners that we work with regularly?

Does the company offer coaching? Very few companies do. Coaching from an experienced professional who has walked the ground you want to travel is invaluable. To have a coach who will hold you accountable for performing the activities that will lead you to success can dramatically shorten and flatten the learning curve. A true coaching program will give you personal attention instead of only a group experience of seminars and workshops. It should be structured and regular in nature, either weekly or twice monthly. It should focus on helping you acquire the sales skills needed to succeed. Your coach should have been a successful agent and have used what she is teaching you. A number of times I have watched agents with passion, desire, commitment, and the right coach to guide them become top agents in the company. Find out more about coaching in chapter 6.

Training and Money

In sales the money you earn is poor if you are simply an average-skilled salesperson. The money you earn improves to average when you are a good salesperson. The income you earn is good when you are a great salesperson. Finally, the money you earn is amazing when you are an outstanding salesperson. The biggest increase in pay is between a great salesperson and an outstanding salesperson. It can mean the difference between earning $100,000 to $200,000 a year for a great salesperson and $500,000 to $1,000,000 a year for an outstanding salesperson. Having coached a lot of agents in the outstanding category, I can tell you that there is a dramatic difference between those outstanding salespeople and the national average income the National Association of Realtors reports for real estate agents, which is $17,000 per year. That's why I say evaluate the training more heavily than the other categories. Your training will determine how high you can go and the income you achieve in real estate sales.

It's Your Decision

There are many choices in life you have to make. Selecting the right company to start your career ranks only behind whom you marry. If you apply these steps and ask questions, you will select the right company for you and be on your way to a great career in real estate.

Getting Off to the Right Start

Y ou have found the right company and your excitement level is at an all-time high. You are entering a new phase in your life: the phase of self-management, self-discovery, and self-motivation to achieve your goals and dreams. Unlike in most other careers, what happens in your real estate career depends totally on you. You are the one who controls the outcome and your destiny. That first day you feel like Leonardo DiCaprio on the bow of the *Titanic* with the wind in your face, screaming, "I am the king of the world!" You are master of all you can see; however, just as in the movie *Titanic*, there are icebergs out there that can end this wonderful new voyage you are on.

This chapter is focused on getting your new adventure off to that start you desire, from your first day, your first week, your first month on the job. What has happened before you get to this point is not as important as what is going to happen from now on. The first step is to forget your past failures. You are staring at a blank slate—you and only you will decide what you are going to write on the slate. Robert Schuller, the famous minister, said, "If it's to be, it's up to me." That is your new mantra. You have ability and talent, and when you mix them with passion and white-hot desire, miraculous things will happen in your career. You are the determining factor of success.

Get Ready for a New Kind of Exam

The first few days of your career will probably be spent in classroom training. When I entered real estate, I had been out of school for many years. I was certainly out of practice in taking notes and organizing thoughts on a lecture for use at a later date. Your first few days, and even your first month, are going to be full of cramming for an exam. This exam is different from the one you took to get your license; it's open book and out in the field. It's not necessarily on paper, but it is about action and results. Your ability to learn and practice the material can make or break your first year in the business. The more time you invest outside of the classroom setting, the quicker your first commission check will come.

Seek Help from the Office Staff

Your first day is going to be filled with just learning where everything is in the office: where all the forms are kept, where the supplies are stored. One great resource to connect with is the administrative staff. Seek to create an alliance with the support staff at the office. Set yourself apart from the other agents by treating the staff with true respect. If the administrative staff has experience, they can be a wonderful resource. They are, after all, the eyes and ears of the real estate company. They often can help you avoid embarrassing situations and they know the procedures that need to be followed. Many will even pitch in to help when you really need it, even if it's not part of their job. Don't neglect to recognize their value. Reaching out for help is just one step in making your new job a positive experience and successful from day one.

Start Early

Your first day is when you must begin to set the tone for your career. If there's one secret that all top real estate agents have, it's that they consider their career a real job, with real, regular hours. Because you have con-

> ## Be There to Pick Up the Keys
>
>
>
> Most companies, IBM for example, require your presence at work at a specific time. In your company, You, Inc., time is far more valuable to your success than it would be if you worked for IBM. The job you have at You, Inc., carries with it the keys to financial independence. Make sure you show up to pick up the keys. Those keys to financial independence are given out early, before most agents arrive in the office. Make sure you are there. Most of the other agents thought I was crazy to go to work so early and even made fun of my work schedule, hours, and commitment. They were not laughing any more when, in my third year, I sold more than 80 properties and became the number one agent in the office. Decide on a time that you will start your workday and don't deviate. A large part of success is showing up regularly.

trol of your time and keep your own schedule, it is very easy to be undisciplined. There were very few mornings in my whole sales career when I was not in the office by seven. I started this habit from day one of my career and it is still with me today. We need to treat our arrival at work as we would any other job.

Believe in Yourself

The best of the best in life believe in themselves. Michael Jordan believed to his core that he was the best. His belief and sheer will to win created his enormous success. I read recently about a survey in which professional golfers were asked, "If you had one putt to win a major championship, whom would you pick to putt it?" Almost all of them chose Jack Nicklaus. Why? Because he was the best at the time and had the ability to *will* the ball into the hole.

You must believe you are the best agent for the job. When your confidence goes up, your competence goes up at the same time.

You must drive your belief deep within yourself. It truly is the secret weapon for all peak performers.

Program your mind through affirmations that you are the best. Each day remind yourself, "I am a great salesperson; I am the best agent someone can hire to do the job; I provide exceptional service to my clients." You must drive your belief deep within yourself. It truly is the secret weapon for all peak performers. Work to improve your belief in yourself. We all came from the same creator, who didn't create any junk. You have it inside you to be exceptional. The secret edge is belief. As Dr. Norman Vincent Peale states:

> Believe in yourself! Have faith in your abilities. Without a humble but reasonable confidence in your own powers, you cannot be successful or happy. . . . Formulate and stamp indelibly on your mind a mental picture of yourself succeeding. Hold the picture tenaciously; never permit it to fade. Your mind will seek to develop the picture.

Understand the Game You Are Playing

Peak performers understand the game they are playing and how to score and win. The game of real estate is about skills, knowledge, and time—these are the three things you are really selling. The better you are at controlling them, the more revenue you can generate and the more time you will have for the other areas of your life.

Perseverance + Belief + Desire = Success

When you add belief to the desire that you already possess and sprinkle in perseverance, the results are magical. A friend of mine, Froy Candelairo, who sells homes in the Los Angeles area, is a perfect example that all who persevere and have a desire can have success in real estate. Froy came to the United States many years ago by hanging on to the underside of a train. He and a friend were trying to get to the United States, the land of opportunity, from Mexico. They rode for hours, clinging to the train for their lives. They had no idea where they were and they could not let go for fear of being run over by the train. The miles clicked by and they were getting extremely tired. Finally, Froy's friend could not hang on any longer. He let go and was crushed. Froy was devastated by the loss of his friend, but vowed to hang on. Less than five minutes later the train stopped. Froy had reached his goal. He had made it to the United States.

Let me finish Froy's story. Froy decided to sell real estate. He had to learn English, pass the real estate licensing requirements, and then find a broker. Froy's passion and desire to succeed were unparalleled. He worked diligently to learn and improve his skills. Today, Froy is one of the most successful agents in the country, selling more than 400 properties a year. The lesson that Froy learned from his immigration experience is that one component of success is being able to hang on a little bit longer than the next guy. Now, if Froy, with all his limitations, could accomplish what he has, you certainly can create a business that will generate the income that you desire.

One of the big challenges for new agents is not turning into 7-day-a-week wonders, where you are on call for clients 24 hours a day, 7 days a week. It is an agent's ability to control her time, while increasing skills and knowledge, that will prevent falling into that trap. You must clearly understand the stark reality of the real estate business: Your compensation is a direct result of your performance. You will get paid at the transfer of the property, and anything less is not a commission check.

You must clearly understand the stark reality of the real estate business: Your compensation is a direct result of your performance.

Acquire a Winning Mindset

One of the key characteristics of successful people is a winning mindset. They have learned to program their minds for success. That's what gives them the edge in competitive situations. This mindset allows them to hit the winning shot at the buzzer, sink the crucial putt on the last hole to win a tournament, or get the listing signed even when they are up against the best agents in town. The question is, why do some people have it and others don't? How can you ensure that you acquire the winning mindset? Let me take you through the development of a winning mindset.

Record and Replay the Tape

Now, I don't mean that you have to record yourself on a tape recorder, but you *do* need to write down and track your victories. We all have a lot of victories daily, weekly, and monthly—we just have a hard time remembering them. If you record them, they can be reviewed during the challenges or rough times. When you lose self-confidence, you can build it back up by reviewing your past triumphs. A lot of our victories come out of very challenging problems or struggles. By taking a look back at your accomplishments and achievements, you will see the direct correlation between the challenges faced and resulting triumphs. The key is to review them regularly. If you do so, they will pay dividends today and tomorrow.

Focus and Stay Positive

Having a successful career in real estate means being able to stay positive and focused on your goals even when all things, people, and conditions are telling you to do otherwise. Make the goal right now to *persevere through the challenges.* Your first year in this business will be your toughest. There will be many times when you feel like you are working hard with no results in sight. Resolve to continue to move forward to improve your skills, learn from your mistakes, and stay focused on your goals. Don't accept the naysayer's view that it can't be done. Keep your mindset positive and directed to success and achieving your objectives. Henry Ford said, "If you think you can or you think you can't, either way, you're right." Ford knew that your belief and mindset will help produce the results that you desire. Staying positive, every day, is one of the hardest parts of sales for any professional.

> *Henry Ford said, "If you think you can or you think you can't, either way, you're right."*

Pick Your Companions Carefully

Concern yourself with what you think is right, and not with what the other agents think. If I had listened to everyone else, I would not have enjoyed the same success early in my career. Evaluate carefully who you allow to influence your thinking.

Avoid the Coffeepot and Donut Bunch

The coffeepot and donut bunch is in every office. They will be there to teach you how to achieve mediocrity in sales. This group is the easiest to spot, and they are always looking for new recruits. They are more than willing to teach you how to do it and may try to impress you with "I've been in the business X years." All that this means is that they have one year's experience X times over. They have very little to offer a new agent with energy and passion. Flee from that group because they will slowly suck you in and drain your tank.

Steer Clear of Negative Thinkers

It's easy to pick up the wrong ideas and knowledge by hanging around the wrong people. Be extremely selective and careful whom you let into your world. I adopted a rule when I started real estate sales that I still use today: Hang out only with people you can learn from, profit from, or have fun with. Those three types of people help you construct an abundant life. The complainers and lemon-suckers will only pull you down to their level. There is an age-old question: How do you keep a crab from climbing out of a bucket? Answer: You just put in another crab; when one tries to crawl out, the other will pull him back down. Some people in a real estate office are like that. Your objective the first week is to find out who those people are and avoid them as if your family and career depended on it (because they do).

I adopted a rule when I started real estate sales that I still use today: Hang out only with people you can learn from, profit from, or have fun with.

Do the Opposite

One rule I learned early in my career that has helped me immensely was the 180 degree rule. The 180 degree rule states that whatever the average agent is doing, do the exact opposite. The average real estate agent makes $17,000 per year, which isn't exactly a smashing success. If you do only what average agents do, you will earn what they earn and achieve what they achieve. Don't think like an average agent; you are better than that.

Invite a Top Agent to Lunch

On your first day find out who are the top agents in the office. You especially want to meet the agents who are most successful in taking listings. These are the agents who have a more stable business year after year. They are the ones you want to hang around, learn from, and profit from.

When you have the opportunity, introduce yourself and ask if you can buy them lunch. You will learn more over that one-hour lunch than you will learn in six months with the coffeepot and donut bunch. Try to schedule a lunch as quickly as possible, preferably that week. If they put you off, keep asking. They'll eventually go. It is hard to resist an eager, hard-charging new agent, and it is actually refreshing to see someone take his career so seriously. If you have more than one "top gun" listing agent in your office, go individually with each one.

Identify People You Want to Be with

Some people fit into all three of my categories: You can learn from them, profit from them, or have fun with them. These are ideal companions, but most people will fit into only one category. Be prepared to enjoy the results of being around people even if they fit into only one category. I have people in my life who are just plain fun to be with. When I spend time with them, we just have fun and laugh. There are other people whom I learn from. This is the group I want to be around all the time. They will lead me to growth, self-improvement, and wealth more than any other group. Your ability to identify this group of people and figure out how to spend more and more time with them is critical to your success.

Share Your Knowledge and Skills

I have added a fourth category of people to hang out with: people I can teach and have an impact on. The greatest joy in my life is to instruct. I love to watch people grow and prosper. The best thing about teaching is that it dramatically improves your skill level in the subject you are teaching. I know more about real estate sales from teaching and coaching for the last handful of years than I learned in my entire sales career. There also is a great joy in the teaching process. Become successful in any field and you will be able to share in that joy. As a new agent, your objective should be to get skilled enough in what you do so you can teach it to someone. I certainly feel blessed for the honor of being able to teach and positively impact people's lives.

Enjoy Other People's Success

I recently had a call with one of my clients. He talked about how his life had changed and how he had listed 12 homes in the last month. He went into detail about the challenges and objectives of each listing appointment and how he overcame them. Then he went on to describe in detail the three buyers who purchased from him in the last week and the five listings that sold that month. After 30 minutes or so, he stopped and realized he had been talking the entire time about how much he had accomplished and how his life had turned around. He was embarrassed to have spent so much time describing the excitement that was going on within his life and had failed to ask how I was doing. He began to apologize for being insensitive. I told him not to be concerned, that I received more enjoyment hearing about how he has reaped the fruits of our work together than from anything else.

There is no greater gift in life than the ability to teach and change someone's life for good. There is no greater honor than to share in the transformation of someone's life. I truly receive no greater joy in life than hearing these stories.

How Your First Days Will Go

We've covered the mindset, attitude, and approach you must have as you begin your new career. But what about the actual job? How will you start? Where will you start? How can you keep all of this new information organized? Following are the answers to these questions as well as what your initial responsibilities will be as a first-year real estate agent.

Learn to Use Listing Contracts and Sales Contracts

Both sellers and buyers are making a huge decision, and your job is to help them feel comfortable doing it. You can facilitate this by assuring them that you are the best agent for the job—and that's hard to do with your head buried in a contract.

The first things you will learn are how to prepare a listing contract and a sales contract—two documents that are essential to your success. You will learn these documents inside-out, which gives you the ability to converse and write at the same time and guide your client to the sale on the buyer side or to a representation relationship on the listing side. Your ability to fill out these forms while conversing with the client will enable you to put their minds at ease. In order to accomplish this feat, you must be intimate with these agreements. You must know what every line and box and space is meant for and why to check it or not check it. Whether you leave a box blank or check it can mean the difference between the seller keeping the refrigerator or the buyer receiving it in the sale, or whether the seller pays the $5,000 in closing costs or the buyer pays for them. The ability to accurately complete the agreement is critical to your success.

Practice in a Safe Place

To ensure your success in this area, you must practice. There are many things in life that we must do a certain number of times before we are skilled at them. When you first got on a bike you probably didn't take right off down the street, and more than likely, you fell down a few times. Thus, you were probably allowed to ride only in a controlled environment, like a backyard. And regardless of natural ability, you had to ride the bike many times before perfecting it.

Real estate sales is no different. You have to practice in a controlled environment, without clients. You will make mistakes in the beginning, and it is better to make them in the backyard than in front of prospects or clients. You must practice to be prepared, and you have a choice: Practice on people who can buy or sell (and possibly

Mastering Paperwork: Four Easy Steps

1. **Find a partner who is willing to help you, someone who has great knowledge of contracts and agreements.** Your broker or manager would be an excellent choice because she has a vested interest in your completing the paperwork correctly.

2. **Review all the paperwork, study every line of the document.** As you are reviewing the paperwork, write down on a legal pad any questions you have. Review both the listing agreement and the sales agreement used in your area. Often each company, or even each board, has its own agreement. If there is anything you are even remotely unsure about, ask. Ignorance is not an excuse when you are dealing with most people's single largest investment.

3. **Have your partner (your broker or whoever is helping you) assign you homes off of the multiple listing service to list and sell, with certain scenarios attached to them.** If you are representing the buyer, have your partner assign you a sales price or down payment. You'll need to practice such details as buying personal property, early possession, long closing date, and seller keeping possession for a certain number of days after closing. You may also encounter complications such as a well, septic tanks, and property disputes. There is an endless list, and you need to know all of the possibilities. Familiarize yourself with every one. Then write the contract for this phantom buyer on paper. Have your partner check your language on the agreement. Did you get all the boxes and spaces filled out completely? Did you cross all the t's and dot all the i's?

4. **Review each contract and listing agreement with others.** Don't leave to chance the responsibility to protect your client. It's too important.

This process should be repeated daily for your first month or two in the business. It will give you the confidence to do the job for the client. The more times you have walked through the contracts before you do it live, the easier it will be when the pressure is really on. When you do your first sales agreement with a client, your heart will be pounding out of your chest. You will sweat like you just ran a marathon, but because you practiced well you won't make a mistake. You will still feel uncomfortable, but errors will not be there.

lose listings, sales, and referrals along the way), or practice on your spouse, children, or other agents in a role-play format to more quickly receive competence. This is true in all areas of the selling process, from paperwork to scripts, dialogues, and presentations.

Sales Scripts and Dialogues

Another type of training you must embrace during your first few weeks is that of sales scripts and dialogues. Your commitment to master these will mean the difference between being a big success with a six-figure income or being out of business before the year is out.

Raise the Comfort Level

Many think having a script is manipulating the sale. I think creating a script is part of being completely prepared. Clients who

Child's Play

At a point in each of our lives we all had tremendous sales skills—and we did not even know it. We intuitively learned and perfected our presentation to the highest level. We persistently pushed forward and never took no for an answer, or at least without a fight, but we usually wore our opponent down and got the sale. We had it all going for us, we had it all figured out, and then we stopped.

Most of us stopped being great salespeople around 10 or 11 years old. Up until that point we were highly skilled salespeople. Have you ever watched children younger than 10 at the store? Most are very good salespeople. The highest skilled are the 3- to 6-year-olds. They know what they want, and they do not take no for an answer. They usually manage to sell their parents on their idea.

Why are they highly skilled? Because they know their scripts and dialogues. They know what to say to get their parents to do what they want. Agents must also have scripts and dialogues to elicit the desired response from the client. Successful agents need to have scripts for sellers and scripts for buyers. Brokers need scripts for other agents and for staff. The better you define what you are going to say, the more successful in saying it you will be.

hesitate in a selling situation may be saying that they need a few more facts to make them feel comfortable. The agent's job is to give clients

Scripting can help the client at the highest level by accurately communicating, in a convincing fashion, the benefits of a particular decision.

the data to help them make the decisions that are best for them. Scripting can help the client at the highest level by accurately communicating, in a convincing fashion, the benefits of a particular decision. To be well-scripted is to be prepared to help the client evaluate the situation carefully by weighing all sides less emotionally. An agent who is well-scripted has a ready response for any given situation. A well-scripted agent has practiced and prepared for the question before it is asked.

Many Professionals Use Scripts

Many professionals in other fields are well-scripted. Professional football teams often have the first 25 to 30 plays of the game planned. They know exactly which plays they will run. They will evaluate how the plays work and continue to use the best ones the following week. Other well-scripted professionals include defense attorneys—many use the same argument this week that worked to get their client acquitted last week; surgeons, who look at X rays and books to perfect upcoming procedures; and pilots, who take off and land their plane the same way every time, according to script. They have all scripted out what they are going to say and do. As well, real estate agents need to be at that level of professionalism, and you must have expert knowledge of your script.

The Power of Scripts

The following sidebar is a short list of the scripts agents must use to be skilled at the delivery of the information they need to provide to buyers, sellers, agents, and affiliates. To join those successful agents, you must learn to develop and deliver scripts with effectiveness. If you do, there will be no cap to your income. The different scripts will not change nor will the basic questions, problems, objections, and solutions. Once you learn to effectively cover these areas, you will be unstoppable. There are not many new objections created by buyers and sellers annually. If you have learned all the objections and can deliver your response to the objections well, you will be rewarded. You may need to make modifications and practice them regularly, but you will not have to go through the process of learning 40 to 50 new scripts and dialogues. The difference between the amateur and the professional in all things is skill and delivery. Anyone can throw a football, but

> ## A Script for Any Occasion
>
>
>
> Agents need scripts for many occasions:
>
> - **Prospecting:** past clients, expireds, FSBOs, cold calls, door knocking, apartment renters, and referral clients
> - **Buyers:** ad calls, sign calls, the right house, qualifying the buyer, commitment to work with you, open houses, and for all objections
> - **Sellers:** listing presentations, qualifying, price reductions, weekly communication, and for all objections
> - **Other agents:** getting them to do their job, creating urgency, showing your properties, and negotiating
> - **Affiliates:** sending more referrals and taking over more functions

he cannot throw it like John Elway without dedication and practice. Elway has perfected his skill with long, hard practice.

Professional salespeople have perfected their delivery of words. They have practiced how to overcome all the objections. They have practiced how they will list a home. Many of us make new presentations every time we go out. That would be like Elway drawing the game plan in the dirt in the huddle every time. How effective would that be?

Do not be put off by poor salespeople who have poor delivery. Scripts and dialogues are often knocked because of poor delivery. Tremendously skilled salespeople are well-scripted; you just cannot tell they are speaking from a script. Constant practice makes the difference.

Computer Training

Another area you must address in your first week is the beginning of your computer training. As a new agent, you will be faced with *multiple listing service computer programs*. These programs allow you to search for properties to show your buyers. They also allow you to determine the value of a home you are hoping to list. There has been more advancement in these programs in the last few years than in the previous 10 years. Using the software to leverage your time is essential.

Prospect Matching Programs

One feature that many programs have, but is not used by many agents, is *the prospect matching* function. That's where you can input the needs and desires of your buyers and the system will notify you when a property that matches your client's needs comes on the market. This feature allows you to provide greater service to your clients with less of your personal time invested. In some boards, this prospect matching can automatically e-mail your client about the property and give a virtual tour of the home. We have to be masters of this software for our clients and our time.

Contact Management Software

The software that is most important will be your contact management software, the lifeblood of your business. The better you know and use this tool, the more money you will make. This software will help you keep track of your leads, past clients, sphere, and all your contacts in this business. Your ability to create and keep a solid database will cause your growth to explode in this business. I have a saying that "money doesn't grow on trees; it grows in databases." Some companies have multiagent databases that you can use. Others require you to provide your own. Whichever is the case, you must learn this tool.

Your ability to create and keep a solid database will cause your growth to explode in this business.

There are many contact management programs available especially for real estate agents, such as Top Producer, Online Agent, ACT!, and Goldmine. Whatever you have available to you, learn it! If you need to purchase one, do so and take the time to learn it. If you have the opportunity to take a few classes where there is an instructor to teach you, do so. There is nothing better than getting live training on the actual program you are using. In live training you will have someone looking over your shoulder while you are working on the program, teaching and coaching you to master every click.

Set Aside Time for Training

Another way to learn is to set aside 30 minutes daily just to work in the software. Plan to spend a certain amount of uninterrupted time learning how to enter prospects, how to create follow-up programs for your leads, and how to keep in touch with your sphere and past clients. There is a large learning curve on the software we must master as real estate agents. The commitment to learn it begins the moment you step in the office for the first time. Remember, the contact management software is the lifeblood of your business. Make sure you are investing the necessary time to master it.

Organization

To create and run your multimillion dollar sales company takes organization. The ability to organize your paperwork, your leads and prospects, and most importantly, your time is essential. If you can learn to control these key areas you will be able to generate a six-figure income.

Take Control of Your Time

The most important of the areas we must control is time because it is the only asset we have where we don't know how much we have. We know what's in our checking or savings account. (For many of us that's not very much and that's why you are entering real estate.) We treat our money with far more care and reverence than our daily time account. An unknown author describes time this way:

> If you had a bank that credited your account each morning with $86,000—that carried over no balance from day to day—and allowed you to keep no cash in your account . . . and every evening cancelled whatever part of the amount you had failed to use during the day—what would you do? Draw out every cent, of course! Well, you do have such a bank—its name is "time." Every morning it credits you with 86,000 seconds . . . every night it rules off as lost whatever of this you have failed to invest to good purposes. It carries over no balance. . . . It allows no overdrafts. Each day it opens a new account for you. If you fail to use the day's deposit, the loss is yours. There is no going back. There is no drawing against tomorrow. You must live in the present—on today's deposit.

We each have the same set amount daily. None of us has more than 24 hours for use that day. Your time needs to be treated as the most precious asset you own. The amount of money we earn is based on our skill and time effectiveness. Poor use of time always equals poor income.

If you want to know the value of a single second, ask the man who lost the Olympic gold medal in the 100-meter race by less than a second. The winner receives millions in endorsements; the loser gets nothing; we don't even remember his name.

Have you ever called your attorney to ask a question and not received a bill for his time? As real estate agents, we too are selling our time and our knowledge. Those are the assets we sell daily. The better you control your time, the more income you will make. Resolve to let no one take time from you without compensation.

Plan for Tomorrow Today

Let me give you a couple of quick strategies for maximizing your time. First, we need to plan for tomorrow before we leave today. Never start a day before you have it planned out on paper. It is really easy for the time to slip away in real estate sales. There are so many people and activities trying to get your attention that you can arrive at the end of the day having produced little to nothing.

The best remedy is to clearly know your tasks and objectives for the day. Great agents *create* their day and what happens; most agents *react* to their day and what happens. There is a huge difference between creation and reaction. In creation you are in control, while in reaction everyone and everything else is in control. Most people have poor time-planning procedures. If they have not planned well for themselves, I can assure you they have planned nothing for you. You are the only person who can plan for you. Start every day with a plan to wring the most out of the day.

> *Great agents* create *their day and what happens; most agents* react *to their day and what happens.*

Prioritize Your Objectives

Once you have the objectives for the day, prioritize them. Create an order of most important to least important. Then when you begin your day, focus on number one on the list. By giving 100 percent of your attention to number one and working at it until it is complete, you will be able to accomplish much more than the average agent. There is an old adage, "You save ten minutes of execution for every one minute of planning." That's a tremendous return on your investment of time.

Organize Your Prospecting

For a new agent, number one on your list is prospecting. Your diligence and focus on daily prospecting is essential to your success.

The best way to ensure consistent sales is to prospect daily.

Eighty percent of all businesses that fail do so because they lack sales. The best way to ensure consistent sales is to prospect daily. We will discuss prospecting in detail in chapter 8. For now, just remember that, for a new agent, prospecting is number one and it must be done daily. Organizing your leads and prospects allows you to know who they are and how often to call. Many agents lose more leads and prospects than they convert. Lack of conversion can be connected to the efficiency of one's organization of leads and prospects.

Create Lead Sheets

Create a lead sheet that has the information and the questions that need to be asked for all prospects and leads. Keep these sheets well organized in a file system based on motivation. Motivation is the gauge of how quickly someone has the desire to do something. The more motivated the client, the quicker they will buy or sell. The goal for agents should be to prospect regularly to generate the most motivated clients. These motivated clients will list their home at a fair market value rather than overpricing their property. We are not looking for prospects who want to test the market. We are looking for people who want to sell now! We are not looking for people who want to shop for the best deal. We are looking for people who want to buy now! By organizing and controlling your leads you will be able to determine the best leads and focus on them most. Keep your leads organized and in front of you at all times.

Organize Your Paperwork

Lastly, organize your desk area for your paperwork. If you have a file drawer, separate it into listings and sales. Keep the sellers separate from the buyers. Establish a folder for each transaction. Don't lump all your paperwork in one folder. If you list a home for sale and then sell that seller a new home, make sure to create two separate folders.

There are many different types of folders to use. I like best the folders that have space on the outside to put transaction information. If your company does not provide them, find another source that does. Often, a title or escrow company will have them available to you free of charge. A company called NEBS sells excellent real estate listing folders in both legal size and standard 8½ × 11 size. You can access NEBS at www.nebs.com or call them at 1-800-225-6380. The more organized you are when it comes to your files, the less time you will need to invest in the administration side of your business.

Organization is critical only because you want to spend the least amount of time servicing and most amount of time prospecting for new transactions. Most agents spend less than 20 percent of their time in prospecting and lead follow-up. These are the activities that generate the revenue; the more time in them, the more money made. Take the time to set up your administration right the first time. It will save you in the long run. The next step is to build a strong relationship with your broker or manager.

Creating a Relationship with Your Manager

3

Most brokers and managers do not expect a new agent to walk in the door and light up the sale board. They do expect you to work diligently and daily to find business and improve your skills. When beginning the training process with new agents, the excitement is high and the anticipation is great. Your broker or manager is going to make the investment in you because he believes you have what it takes to succeed. He is willing to invest his time and resources into helping you achieve your dreams. As in any relationship, there will be challenges at times with your broker or manager. There will be times when your performance does not meet the other's expectations. How you talk through it and create specific action plans to improve your performance is essential.

Your Manager Is on Your Side

The relationship you have with your manager can be anything you create it to be. It can be cooperative and mentoring or adversarial and combative. The key is ongoing communication between you and your manager.

I have never met a manager who would not be willing to do whatever it takes for her agent to succeed, provided the agent is willing to put in more effort than the manager.

Many people have the attitude that if the stove would only give them a little heat, then they would put in the wood. Life does not work that way. We have to build the fire before we get the heat.

Zig Ziglar said, "Life is like a cafeteria line . . . first you pay and then you get to eat." You will be amazed how many people will help you if you start first and keep going.

When you are willing to pay the price, many people will join to help you all along the way. Your manager will be leading the charge.

Your career and the quality of your training are entirely up to you; you have the keys to success clearly in your possession.

What You Bring to Your Training

This initial period is a critical time for you to get from your broker or manager what you need to succeed. Your obligation is to stay focused, excited, energized, and grateful for the opportunity you have been given. If you don't exude those characteristics, your manager will eventually lose interest in training you.

Your career and the quality of your training are entirely up to you; you have the keys to success clearly in your possession. Your manager will help you use the keys better and quicker. It is up to you to bring them to the office every day. It is up to you to keep these keys shiny and ready to be used at a moment's notice. As a coach and speaker, I will go the extra mile for the people who come to me for help with their two keys ready. Most successful brokers feel the same way; they will go all out to help new agents who have a great attitude and positive expectations.

Attitude and expectation—these are the key concepts that lead to success. They affect the successful outcome of your business, your marriage, and many other areas of your life. Although you may have incredible talent and skill, you will fail if you do not master these two concepts. Even if you have limited talent and skill, you will win if you live by these two power words. They will determine your future.

If you have a positive, forward-looking attitude, you will accomplish great things. How is your attitude? Does it need improvement? Are you positive and upbeat? If you believe that every challenge or obstacle leads to new opportunity, success is all but guaranteed.

Build a Positive Attitude

Excel with Attitude

When we hire people at Real Estate Champions, attitude is the first and most important characteristic we look for in a team member. An employee with a great attitude will learn the skills needed to excel.

If Life Gives You Lemons, Make Lemonade

Thomas Edison was said to have been motivated to create the electric light bulb because darkness interfered with his ability to conduct further experiments. He wanted to be able to work long into the night. Edison could have moaned about the darkness. That would not have accomplished anything. Instead, he used his positive attitude and solved the problem of darkness. There are thousands of examples in life of how some people took lemons and, with a great attitude, made lemonade.

Start building your attitude today. Convince yourself that you are the best agent anyone could hire. You have to be convinced yourself before anyone else will be convinced. The attitude you bring to objections will help you handle them and get the contract signed. The attitude that you take when you have a problem transaction will make the difference between a closing and a deal falling through.

Exhibit Unshakeable Confidence

The second power word is expectation. If you don't expect to win, you will not win. If you go on a listing and expect to take it at your price and commission, you will. If you go expecting a fight on commission and your price, you will receive that also.

Set the positive expectation of success before the appointment with a prospect or client. You also need to set a positive expectation before every phone call you make. Expectation is the gateway to confidence.

The first step to having unshakeable confidence is to believe you are the agent for the job. If your expectation is strong enough people will come around to your way of thinking. You just need to be stronger in will and mental focus than clients, prospects, and other agents are.

Your expectation will create your reality. You have to expect before you can receive. You need to envision the people and situations that will enable you to create the future you desire. Expectation does not mean you don't have to work. In fact, you will work harder than before to develop the outcome you desire.

I Am a Great Salesperson

To improve your attitude, use affirmations. Affirmations drive positive mental pictures into your subconscious mind.

- I am a great salesperson.
- I am skilled at handling objections and getting the contract signed.
- People do business with me because I am positive, knowledgeable, and professional.
- I will earn _____ (you fill in the blank).

Use these affirmatives or create your own to improve your mental attitude daily.

The Role of Failure in Your Career

Expectation takes away the fear of failure. Failure is a natural part of success—don't let it paralyze you. You cannot have success without failure. The exhilaration of success would be lost without the frustration of failure. Most people forget the failures over time and remember only the victories. Take Babe Ruth, for example—he hit the most home runs of his time. He also had the most strikeouts. No one remembers that . . . only the home runs . . . the successes.

Babe Ruth hit the most home runs of his time. He also had the most strikeouts. No one remembers that . . . only the home runs . . . the successes.

Your Manager Can Help You Achieve Success

One of the roles of a manager is to help you achieve your dreams. Since she should know the path to success, she should be able to move you toward it quicker. What your manager does not know is what success is to you, what your dreams are for your new career, and what price you are willing to pay.

For your manager to hold you accountable for the dreams and goals you have set, you need to share them with her. I can guarantee that there is not a manager alive who possesses the ability of Carnac. Carnac was a character, created by Johnny Carson on the

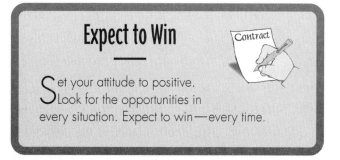

Expect to Win

Set your attitude to positive. Look for the opportunities in every situation. Expect to win—every time.

Winning Is an All Time Thing

Vince Lombardi said:

Winning is not a sometime thing; its an all time thing. You don't have to win once in a while, you don't do things right once in a while, you do them right all the time. Winning is a habit, unfortunately so is losing.

Lombardi had the right attitude and the right expectations. He believed he would win—every time.

Tonight Show, who could read what was in a sealed envelope when he held it next to his head. Your manager needs to know your goals and dreams so a plan can be designed for you to achieve them.

Set Clear Objectives

I recently read a statement by Oliver Wendell Holmes. He said, "To reach the port of success, we must sail; sometimes

Overcome the "Impossible"

Many years ago Henry Ford went to his engineers and told them to build a V-8 engine. They said it could not be done. Ford told them plainly to go do it and report back in 90 days. When the 90 days were up, they again met with Ford. The engineers had spent the whole 90 days dwelling on why a V-8 engine was impossible. They tried to convince Ford it could not be done—a V-8 engine was impossible and could never be created. Ford's attitude and expectation of a V-8 engine were stronger than the engineers' attitude and expectation that it could not be done. We all know who won in the end.

with the wind, and sometimes against it, but we must sail, not drift or lie anchor." To be adrift is to be without specific goals and objectives. We must be clear and focused on where we are heading. This quotation has led me to develop the image of sailing toward a successful life. The first step for a successful sailor is to have a specific port he is trying to reach. We who seek a successful life must also have an objective. The objective must be clear and concise, crystallized, and definite.

Objectives Versus Goals

Too often, we are very fuzzy about our main objective in life. Our main objective is beyond what we do. It's beyond the income, sales, and money we earn. It's beyond our business and all the challenges that surround it. Too often the objective is monetary. To earn X amount of dollars or sell so many homes, in my perspective, is not the main objective in life. It at best is a goal to be obtained along the way. The desired end is not the money itself. It could be what the money could do for us or the lifestyle it allows us to enjoy.

Your Key Supporters

You have set a specific target and, in order to achieve it, you need other people to hold you accountable. The two most logical people to keep you accountable are your spouse (or significant other) and your manager. Those two will have the greatest impact on the achievement of your objectives besides you. I can clearly state that I would not have had as successful a real estate sales career without my wife, Joan. She has played an incredible role in my success each and every day. My manager was also a key supporter. He was always supportive, encouraging, and willing to share his wisdom. For either of them to help guide and motivate me, they needed to clearly understand my goals and objectives.

"To reach the port of success, we must sail; sometimes with the wind, and sometimes against it, but we must sail, not drift or lie anchor."
Oliver Wendell Homes

View the Difficulty As an Advantage

One of the hardest tasks in life is to set that clear objective. If it were easy, everyone would do it; everyone would achieve success. But we are often stopped by the difficulty of the task. The difficulty should be viewed as an advantage. Now that's a novel mindset, isn't it? The more difficult the task, the fewer the people who will master it. The fewer people who have mastery, the lower the level of competition. Few people have mastered success. That's why there is so much opportunity.

Studies have shown that the peak earning years for people are in their 50s and early 60s. For many it takes that long to master success. It takes years of trial and error to get it right. Most people never hit the mark or get it right. If we are progressing, learning, and moving forward, we are successful . . . provided we have a definite aim or objective.

Money Does Not Make a Millionaire

One of my favorite speakers is Jim Rohn. Jim says that it's not the money that makes the millionaire. It is what that person became in order to attract the million dollars. What is truly valuable are the skills, mindset, discipline, and character the person developed on the way to that objective. The money is fleeting, but the skills of character, mindset, and discipline last forever.

Make the Most of Favorable Winds

The second key point in the Oliver Wendell Holmes quotation is the concept of "against the wind or with the wind." There will be days when things go smoothly and we are with the wind. We are hot and everything we touch turns to gold. We gain appointments easily. We create trust effectively with our prospects and clients. The market around the country is responding favorably with listings selling within days. A skilled sailor will sail long and hard on those days. She will ensure that she makes the most miles she can by sailing longer, harder, and with more focus and intensity. How often do we let up when we have things rolling and the momentum is with us? When we have favorable wind, do we take a mental break? Do we let up? That's the time to pour it on!

It's human nature to let up or to ease back on the throttle of success. People often neglect what they did to create the momentum in the first place, but you must not. *Carpe diem . . .* Seize the day. Seize the opportunity when the conditions are favorable.

Focus on the Mainsail in Heavy Weather

There will also be days, weeks, and maybe longer when the wind is against you, when you feel like you are right in the middle of a squall. A highly skilled sailor realizes that this is a passing storm. He may not know the length and breadth of the storm, but it will pass in time. When the storm hits, you need to understand it will move on. You can weather the challenge.

Decide on an objective. Plot the course. Navigate the winds and challenges. Celebrate when you arrive.

A good sailor will also go back to basics in a storm. He will take down the spinnaker; he may remove the jib. He focuses all his attention on the most important thing to get him out of the storm—he focuses on the mainsail.

What's your mainsail in life? What's the mainsail in your business? Do you focus intently on the mainsail in times of trial or are you concerned about the spinnaker? There will always be peripheral stuff in your life and business, but don't take down the mainsail. Keep working the wind. Use your mainsail . . . weather the storm.

Don't Quit

The last essential point is for you not to stop, never quit. Perseverance leads to success. Champions don't stop when they encounter adversity. Like good sailors they keep focused on the objective and don't let the tides drift them off course. You can learn a lot from a skilled sailor. The skills and challenges are the same in sailing as in real estate. Decide on an objective. Plot the course. Navigate the winds and challenges. Celebrate when you arrive.

Create a Plan

Once you have set clear objectives, work with your manager to create a plan to achieve them. Decide on the income you desire for the year. Figure out the number of transactions that you need to achieve your set income goal. Ask your manager what she thinks you need to learn to achieve that goal of income. Together, write down the steps so you can check them off as you go.

Your manager can help keep you on track and focused toward the goals you have set.

Check Your Progress Regularly

Commit to a scheduled time to meet with your manager weekly to check your progress. The best results in life come from consistency of activity. To truly be held accountable, you need a regular time with your manager to check your progress. My friend Zig Ziglar describes this as a "check-up from the neck up." To hit the production and income goal you have set, you can't be going in the wrong direction for a month or even a week. Your manager can help keep you on track and focused toward the goals you have set.

Get in the Game Every Day

To create success, what you know is only the first step. A lot of people know a whole lot, but don't get very far in life. You will be rewarded based on what you do with what you know. We are scored only on action, on doing what we should and need to do. That means that we must act. We can't sit on the sidelines in observation. We have to get in the game every day and apply what we have learned.

Without reaching out and picking up the phone and making the first lead follow-up call or prospecting call, we are assured failure. It is that one motion of picking up and dialing that first number that separates the winner from the loser. In terms of time, less than two seconds will determine your outcome.

You, Inc.

Your career is up to you. You are the one who will create this multimillion dollar business. I truly believe everyone in life is self-employed. You are the owner of your own personal service company. It doesn't matter if you are a real estate agent, doctor, attorney, construction worker, or secretary. In the final analysis, you work for your own company: You, Inc.! At this moment, you may be selling your services to any number of other companies, but ultimately you have to view this whole business you are creating as You, Inc.

You are the president of a wonderful new company that is going to take the real estate industry by storm. This company of yours is going to become a whole new powerhouse in the real estate industry. It is you who controls the success and direction of the company. What you do will lead you to the results you seek.

The First Step

Lao-tzu said, "A journey of a thousand miles begins with a single step." John Maxwell said, "Success is a journey not a destination." Combine the two and create "the successful journey begins with a single step." That is what stops most people . . . that first step. That little step separates abundance from failure. Without that first step you are guaranteed to not accomplish your objective.

The Pain of Discipline Versus the Pain of Regret

Now, I realize that there is some pain involved with lead follow-up and prospecting; however, there is also pain involved if you don't do it. There are two kinds of pain, the pain of discipline (making the lead follow-up and prospecting calls) and the pain of regret. The truth is, we are going to experience one of them—it is impossible not to. You have to choose which you would rather live with. You are the one who ultimately does the choosing.

"All glory comes from daring to begin," according to Eugene Ware.

When we take the step to make the calls, we are experiencing the pain of discipline, the pain of potential rejection, the pain of sacrifice, and the pain of hard work. To avoid the pain of regret you must pursue this course with single-minded purpose. You must decide and commit to the disciplined path. "All glory comes from daring to begin," according to Eugene Ware. If you do not begin, you have selected the pain of regret.

Discipline Becomes Desire

Discipline involves work and commitment. Success is not purchased all at one time, but on the installment plan. We achieve success only through disciplined effort over time. When we make the calls daily to our leads, prospects, past clients, sphere, expireds, and FSBOs, we will achieve success. We will also move far away from the pain of regret. When we create a habit of daily discipline, an almost magical thing happens. One day you will realize that your discipline has turned into desire: the desire to do the calls daily, the wanting to make the calls because of the habit and the results. The road will get easier to stay on.

The pain of discipline will pass and transform into desire. The pain of regret can linger forever.

The pain of discipline we feel now . . . today. We may not feel the pain of regret for hours, days, weeks, months, or years. This will often cause us to make the wrong decision because we would prefer to have no pain now or ever. The pain of discipline will pass and transform into desire. The pain of regret can linger forever. Start today toward discipline and away from regret.

Begin your success journey today with a single step.

Regret

If we don't attack our dreams, we will experience the greatest pain in life, the pain of regret. Sydney Harris wrote, "Regret for the things we did can be tempered by time; it is the regret for the things we did not do that is inconsolable." There will be regret for not doing what we know we should do; regret for not achieving our goals and dreams; regret for not crafting a grand lifestyle for our family and ourselves; regret for not living up to our potential. At what point does potential turn into regret? There is that moment in time. It's different for each one of us. Are you nearing that point?

Do What Needs to Be Done Daily

What happens in You, Inc., can be defined by what needs to happen daily. The most successful people in life are skilled at doing just that, never neglecting to do what needs to be done now. Neglect is one of the key reasons for failure.

True success comes from accomplishing daily the activities that will lead you to your ultimate goals in life. Failing to accomplish the daily disciplines will lead you down the path of lost opportunities and lost income.

If we were zapped today for neglecting daily disciplines rather than in the future, our daily disciplines would change. We need to associate pain today with not doing our daily disciplines in the real estate business. We have to make the neglect more painful than the activity.

Pay Later

If the penalty for not accomplishing your daily activities or disciplines were assessed today, you would look at neglecting those activities differently. The truth is that the penalty for neglect resides more in the future than in today. The person who eats fried foods does not pay the penalty at 35; he pays at 55. The person who fails to save 10 percent of his income for retirement is not penalized at 40, but at 60. The prospecting we fail to do today does not hurt our income today, but 90 to 120 days from now.

Three Disciplines for Success in Real Estate Sales

Three disciplines must be practiced daily in real estate for success—fueling growth, attending to administration, and working on your business.

The more of your day you spend in growth, the more income you will make.

The Power of Commitment to Growth

I have a client named Rich Purvis who lives in Midland, Michigan. Rich is one of the nicest guys you will ever meet. He came to us in March of 2000, frustrated about his career. He had been a part-time agent for a handful of years, but had recently gone full-time after 25 years as a firefighter. He had a solid first year, doing about 19 transactions. We started coaching Rich to help him zero in on his activities and his prospecting.

Rich was focused on making his 10 contacts a day to his sphere and past clients. I can count on one hand how many times he failed to meet his daily contact goals over the past nine months. Those 10 contacts took him roughly an hour to do. By year-end, Rich had almost tripled his income and more than doubled his number of closings.

If you had the opportunity to talk to Rich, he would humbly say that he was not the most skilled agent when he started making the 10 contacts a day. He just made a commitment to the growth area of his business daily. As of this writing, Rich is on track to double his business again this year. How many agents or companies do you know that will more than double their business two years in a row?

Make the decision to spend time daily in the growth area of your business. Your broker will respect and applaud your efforts. Rich's broker is a huge fan because of Rich's discipline. You will achieve the same relationship and respect from your broker by focusing on growth daily.

Fueling Growth

Growth is the part of the business that brings in the revenue. The more of your day you spend in growth, the more income you will make. Most agents focus little time each day on growth activities. They work on growth activities at the last minute, when they are running short on funds. That is too late. To have a steady business income you need a steady approach to growth.

Growth occurs in the prospecting that you do daily. It is in the listing appointments that you have for the day. It is the lead follow-ups that you are doing on the people who want to buy or sell. It is the meeting with your lender to work on your competitive advantage in the marketplace.

Growth is the indispensable part of any business. Without growth a business will fail. I know a lot of agents who are highly skilled in growth and poorly skilled in administration and working on their business who earn large amounts of money. I know of very few successful agents who are not highly skilled at growth. You can have huge deficiencies in administration and working on your business but still win the game. You cannot be deficient in growth and win. At Real Estate Champions our focus is to help our clients achieve a high level of skill in all three areas, but growth is the engine that powers the train—you must first pay attention to growth.

Growth demands a minimum of three hours daily: prospecting, appointments, lead follow-up, and meeting with affiliates. Prospecting should be 65 percent of your growth time daily. If the prospecting does not happen, the other growth areas will wither. Remember, the higher the number of hours spent on growth, the higher your income and profit.

Administrative Activities

These are the activities that complete the income stream:

1. processing the listing so agents can find it in the multiple listing service
2. processing the sold property through escrow
3. communicating with your clients on a regular basis
4. directing your staff and monitoring their progress

Attending to Administration

You will need one to two hours daily for administration. If you create a good system, your time spent in this area will be reduced. In the ideal system administration gets done well, but the agent spends little of his personal time on it.

Working on Your Business

This is the time most people neglect. Working on your business really separates success and growth from just running faster

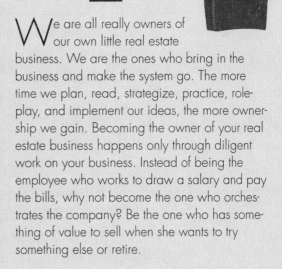

You Own Your Business

We are all really owners of our own little real estate business. We are the ones who bring in the business and make the system go. The more time we plan, read, strategize, practice, role-play, and implement our ideas, the more ownership we gain. Becoming the owner of your real estate business happens only through diligent work on your business. Instead of being the employee who works to draw a salary and pay the bills, why not become the one who orchestrates the company? Be the one who has something of value to sell when she wants to try something else or retire.

Schedule Your Routine Activities

Contract

What do you think your business would look like in 90 days or even 6 months if you were to implement this daily routine?

Growth: 3 hours
Administration: 1 to 2 hours
Business: 1 hour

Schedule these activities into your daily routine. You will be amazed at the results you will achieve, even in 1 week.

Being disciplined is a struggle for every person in life, but it's a lot easier to do a small amount daily and establish a disciplined habit.

on the treadmill of life. Long-term financial success lies in this section of your day. The ability to earn more profit is also located here.

Working on your business is taking a step back from the daily rat race and looking at your growth and administration areas for ways to improve them. Look at your productivity and profitability, then evaluate your progress. You cannot make meaningful change without evaluation as an owner rather than as an employee on a treadmill. Working on your business is essential to moving to the next level of production, decreasing time worked without reducing income, and finding where to cut expenses by 10 percent. Working on your business will help you create economies of scale in administration and new ways to produce growth and income in your business. Plan to spend one hour a day on this.

Do not allow distractions to overtake you and your new daily focus. Do not neglect to do the things that will lead you to success. Do them daily without fail. Being disciplined is a struggle for every person in life, but it's a lot easier to do a small amount daily and establish a disciplined habit. The level of our discipline can often dictate the level of our success.

> ## Great Customer Service Is What the Client Thinks It Is
>
>
>
> ---
>
> Giving great customer service is difficult because each person you are dealing with has his own definition of what great customer service entails. In his book *Selling* (Dove Books, 1996), Mark McCormack describes great customer service this way: "You can be doing the best job in the world for your client but if there's something missing, if the client is unhappy, then all your opinions about your performance are worthless. Great service is a matter of perception. Great service is what the client thinks it is."

Customer Service

Brokers are especially sensitive to customer service. They view poor customer service by any agent as affecting the whole company and the other agents in the company. In the end, they are right. Your ability to create satisfied customers is crucial to the business of You, Inc., as well as the company you work for.

What Does Customer Service Mean to Your Clients?

The first step to providing great customer service is to find out what it means to the customers you are working with now. On the listing appointment ask the sellers these questions:

> Because I desire to provide the highest level of customer service, what are your specific expectations of me?

What are your expectations regarding my communication with you?

What other services can I provide for you?

When you go through their answers you will develop a very clear picture of their definition of customer service. This knowledge will enable you to exceed their expectations and provide exceptional service.

Schedule Contacts Regularly

The second step is to create the procedures that will enable you to provide exceptional customer service. Most consumers equate consistency of communication with customer service. If you agreed to call clients once a week to update them, then do it every week without fail. Schedule the calls in your contact manager software. This reminder will ensure that you make the call. If you agreed to do a written report monthly, block out a few hours once a month to complete all the written reports to your clients. The more automated you become, the more consistently you will be able to provide exceptional service every time.

Lack of communication is the largest complaint consumers

Meet Your Clients' Customer Service Expectations
———

Don't leave to chance your ability to create clients for life. You may get busy and drop the ball mentally. It's easy to overlook your commitments when your life and business are in chaos. Systematize your mailing, phone contacts, and correspondence. It's the only way to ensure the result you and your clients are looking to achieve. Make sure you clearly know the standard they have for customer service. All clients desire to have that standard met. If you can't meet it, refer them to someone who can before you enter into the relationship. Then move on and find other clients.

have against Realtors. Resolve today to start to communicate with your clients weekly or every two weeks. Even if you have nothing to report, you need to check in. Your clients will appreciate that you came through on your commitment to contact them. They will respect you for your integrity of purpose. The most efficient way to do that is through your contact manager software (On Line Agent, ACT, Top Producer, Goldmine, for example). The contact with your clients must be preprogrammed. Note all additional needs of your clients so you can ensure their timely completion.

The Four Rules of Real Estate

There are four rules of real estate. If you apply them each moment of each day, you will have success. You will also build a wonderful relationship with your manager. Your ability to focus on these four will make or break your relationship with your manager and your career.

Learning to focus is one of the most valuable skills you can acquire.

   1. Be there. There is an old saying, "Wherever you go . . . there you are." Now that's a cute little saying, but the truth is most of us have to struggle to live it. How many times have we gone to work or spent time with our family and we weren't really there? We were certainly there in physical body, but were we mentally there? Were we really in the moment as we needed to be?

   "Be there" has two meanings for us as real estate agents. First, be physically there:

- Show up on time. Being on time to a listing appointment can often mean the difference between getting the listing and not getting the listing.

It's Only a Small Detail . . .

It is usually a small detail that separates success from failure. Just ask the United States women's soccer team or better yet, ask China. One penalty kick made the difference between first and second place at the World Cup. The difference between the number one PGA tour player, Tiger Woods, and number 150 is about one stroke per 18 holes and over four million dollars in earnings. Focus mentally on the moment you are in.

- Prepare well before you go on an appointment.
- Treat your real estate career like a real job. Show up at work every day at the same time. My day started at 7 A.M. during my sales career. It was very rare for me not to be in the office at that time.

All Part of the Game

Mark McGwire realizes that striking out is all part of playing baseball. He knows he will have other opportunities. He will have other times at bat, some today and some tomorrow. If a pitch fools him, he learns from it so as not to get fooled again.

We are all going to strike out. We are going to strike out with buyers and sellers, other agents, and our broker. It is just part of life. We must learn from our mistakes and move on.

2. Focus mentally. Second, be there mentally. Be in the moment with intense concentration. The better you focus mentally, the more results you will get for your time invested. If you need to be listening to the client, focus on what the client is saying. If you are formulating your answer or response, you are not listening to the client. Learning to focus is one of the most valuable skills you can acquire. Focus always comes before success. Pay attention to what is happening around you, pay attention to the details of success.

3. Tell the truth. In every situation tell the truth. Agents often have to tell people something they don't want to hear. For example, their home is worth $150,000, but they want $165,000. What do you do? Many agents will take the listing at $165,000 and deal with the $15,000 price reduction later. My belief is that it is better to tell the truth. You may not get the listing, but at least you will know you were honest. Too many of us hedge or shade the truth. Understand there will be a time of reckoning. It may not be now, but it will come. It may be when the market slows and you have a bunch of listings that will not sell.

4. Accept the results and move on. We need to accept the results we get. Work to understand them and the reasons why, and then move on to any necessary changes. If you are worried about the lost deal, you won't be able to focus on the one that is currently in front of you.

Be a Hall of Famer

Lawrence Taylor had a great thought that he shared at his induction into the National Football League Hall of Fame. He said, "A Hall of Famer is not someone who never falls down. A Hall of Famer is someone who continues to pick himself up and gets back into the game after he has fallen down."

Accept the Challenge

It's easy to lie on the ground in the mud when the challenges come at you. There will be times when you feel like lying there—when the buyer you have been working with makes a deal with someone else, when you lose a listing you thought you had, when the deal you have been working for weeks on keeping together finally falls apart despite all your efforts.

Your manager will want to clone you if you apply the ability to be there in all situations, to focus mentally in the moment you are in right now. He will have incredible respect for your telling the truth in all situations and your philosophy to accept the results and move on. You manager has enough people who are blaming others for their lack of success. You commitment to acceptance and improvement will have him firmly behind your success.

Building Relationships with Coworkers

A real estate sales career is an incredibly unique business. It takes a special person to achieve a high level of success in this industry. Successful real estate agents have to wear many hats to be successful. They need the evaluation skills of an analyst, the consulting skills of a psychiatrist, the knowledge of legal contracts of an attorney, and the patience of a saint. Most successful agents also have very high ego strength.

Because of these special skills and the close proximity in which agents work and compete, the relationship with your coworkers is unlike any other in the business world. Gaining and maintaining the competitive edge will create revenue for you. Your ability to understand the game of real estate and put your best competitive foot forward will advance your career quickly.

The structure of the relationship between you and your broker as well as the other agents in the office can sometimes lead to difficulties. In this chapter we discuss the nature of your employment and how that affects competitiveness and cooperation. We also look into strategic partners and how to manage your relationship with them.

The Independent Contractor

The first unique element of the real estate business is your employment status. As a real estate agent, you are an independent contractor. That means that the federal government does not recognize you as an employee. The broker and the company you represent do not actually employ you. You are an independent contractor for the real estate company. For many people entering real estate, this is the first time they have not had an employer.

Real estate agents need the evaluation skills of an analyst, the consulting skills of a psychiatrist, the knowledge of legal contracts of an attorney, and the patience of a saint.

The broker saves a significant amount of money annually due to this type of employment status. You, as the agent, will have to pay for your own insurance and your own self-employment taxes. Self-employment tax status means that you pay the employer a portion of the taxes as well. That amounts to 7.5 percent of the total income you generate. Your broker will give you a 1099 form at the end of the year instead of a W-2. You alone are responsible for saving the money for your taxes.

Competition for Commission Dollars

Independent contractor status can lead to the wrong kind of competition between agents. A lack of cooperation can occur because sometimes you and another agent in your office could be in competition for the same client. This means you are competing for the same commission dollars. I have witnessed first-hand arguments between agents over clients and commission dollars. Agents can get very emotional about their clients and their income since we are all operating without the safety net of a base salary. There is no security in the income you make. Essentially, every day you are unemployed and you have to go out and find a job. There is also no bonus program from the company—the only bonus program is the one that you create daily for yourself. It's you and the phone and your clients and prospects. The pressure is on to perform.

Competition from Outside Your Office

Although there is competition among the agents inside the office for the commission dollar, the greatest competition comes from the agents in other companies. Most successful managers and companies control the negative competition inside their office, but outside the office there is no control. You will run up against some agents who are very cutthroat. They will even do unethical things to try to obtain a client.

Cooperation Among Agents

We walk on a razor's edge as sales people because it really takes all of us to be successful. You might have heard the term *co-op broker*. This is short for cooperating broker. Over 90 percent of the transactions in real estate are done through co-op brokers. We have to compete with each other, but we also have to work with each other. I would not have had the success in my career if not for the other agents in my marketplace helping to sell my listings by showing them to their buyers.

Be Your Client's Advocate

The ultimate goal is to develop cooperation out of a very competitive environment. To achieve a high level of success in real estate, you have to play competitively, play cooperatively, and still be on your client's side. There are times when you must be your clients' advocate above all else. You may have to ruffle the feathers of the other agents and brokers to protect and represent your client properly. You have to be willing to take the negative heat for the benefit of your client.

Diffusing Confrontation

In moments of confrontation or impasse, here is an effective question for any agent, especially a new one:

If you were in my position, what would you do?

This type of question diffuses the confrontation quickly. The agent may give you an insight that you had not yet considered. We can get so focused on our point of view that we never consider another person's. It may also force the other agent to view the conflict from your perspective.

Being able to work in that competitive environment without getting emotionally attached is essential.

The best agents have the objectivity to stand away from a problem transaction and see all the pieces. They don't allow the emotions of all the parties to affect their advice and counsel. They have the ability to view the whole picture as well as each piece of the puzzle that makes up a transaction. Being able to work in that competitive environment without getting emotionally attached is essential. That marks the skill of a tremendous agent. That is also what the clients hire an agent to do.

Stand Your Ground

Too often, agents err by getting too cooperative with others at their own expense. This can cause you to become a push-over for the other agents in the office. Others will lose respect for you over time if you fail to hold your ground. Other agents in the marketplace can often bully a new agent. Don't become intimidated by another agent.

The Importance of Preparation

Personal preparation before each competitive moment is essential. Take the time to prepare before each listing presentation, property showing, offer presentation, or negotiating moment. The time you invest analyzing the value of the home you are going to list or sell creates credibility and confidence in you. Too many agents do not do the preparation necessary to understand the properties and to know the market condition. You can never have too much information.

A final word on preparation for a client is this: Don't

There Is No Second Place

Setting your focus and mindset for winning the listing or closing the sale is paramount in your early career. When I started real estate sales in 1990, my mentality was the same as when I played sports. I was a professional racquetball player for a handful of years in my 20s. I started playing and competing in racquetball tournaments in grade school. My attitude at a racquetball tournament was always, "There is no second place."

My focus was the first place trophy. Anything short of that one mark was failure. I felt the same pain if I lost in the first round of a tournament or if I lost in the finals. To me there was no difference. There was only one trophy and that trophy was first. I was so focused on winning the whole tournament that I was not satisfied with anything else.

That mindset and focus really helped me to achieve in real estate sales. I programmed those thoughts and attitudes into my mind early in my real estate career. I realized early on that in selling real estate "There is no second place."

announce to the world that you are a new agent. The client you are representing doesn't need to know that fact. Furthermore, the other agents you are in competition with do not deserve that information. If you prepare well, they will never know you are in the first year of real estate.

Winning Is the Only Thing

In the game of real estate sales you either get paid or you don't. Selling real estate is like that tough teacher you had in junior high who would not give out partial credit on your exam. She would give you credit only when you got it exactly right. Being a real estate agent is exactly like that. You get compensated only for the whole job—after that deal closes and title changes hands. That's the only place and time you get paid.

The Dead Deal

In coaching sessions, we often hear agents lament about all the work they do just to have the deal fall apart at the eleventh hour. We hear stories every week of how hard someone has worked and then, in one moment, the deal is dead. There are many moments in a real estate transaction when you could finish in second place. The seller might call you after you present a great listing presentation and say, "Susie, we really appreciate your coming out to share how to sell our home with us. We see you are extremely professional. We also think you would do a great job, *but* we have decided to go with someone else." At that moment the fact that you placed second to another agent gives you no comfort. It also provides zero income to you and your family. When you finish in second place enough times it will cause you to close a little harder.

Play to Win

What can you do to make sure you walk out of the listing appointment with the contract signed? Try using more probing questions in your appointments. Focus on handling every step completely and to the best of your ability. As a salesperson you have one moment to make the sale. Are you going to seize that moment? Are you going to push for the tape to win the gold? Now is the time to go for the winning shot!

There is always a critical moment in each selling situation. The question is, "Are you going to recognize it and take advantage of the opportunity?" That moment, and what you do in that moment, will separate first place from second place. Seize that moment. Play to win.

Become Involved in the National Association of Realtors

The National Association of Realtors is one of the most active lobbying groups in the country. A fantastic way to create connections in the real estate community is to become active in your local board. The board is always fighting for your rights as a real estate agent. It lobbies for the rights of the consumer as well. By becoming involved, you will learn a tremendous amount about the career you have selected. You will become more recognized in the real estate community. By gaining recognition, you will improve your impact when dealing with cooperating agents in a transaction. Being recognized as a leader on your board or being a Million-Dollar Club member has its advantages. It gives you

A fantastic way to create connections in the real estate community is to become active in your local board.

extra exposure to the public, your clients, and to the other agents on the board.

Strategic Partners

There are other key coworkers in a real estate agent's career—what I call "strategic partners." There are many professionals who provide services and generate revenue from a real estate transaction. The most common are mortgage originators, attorneys, home inspectors, repair people, and in many states, title companies and escrow companies.

Make Beautiful Music

Just as all members of a quality symphony orchestra perform with precision, you and your mortgage partner need to have that same precision. In a quality orchestra, violins flow with the brass section. The percussion section needs to be aware of its volume and not drown out the other instruments of the orchestra. The conductor will direct and guide the symphony so the desired result will be achieved. If one instrument in the orchestra is flat, the music does not have the same sound or lasting impact on the listener; one instrument can ruin the whole sound instantly. You, the real estate agent, need to take the role of the master conductor if you want to ensure the quality of your product. If one part of the transaction goes flat for your clients, you can lose future referrals from these clients. For many clients, it only takes one sour note to turn them off. Protect your business against that one bad note.

The Mortgage Originator

The most important individual to your career is the mortgage originator. Having your mortgage originator as a key strategic partner can dramatically improve your early real estate career. By being interdependent, the two of you can provide outstanding service.

Being able to work in harmony is essential. Mortgage originators and real estate agents need to work in concert to achieve the beautiful music of satisfied customers. There is nothing more pleasing than a phone call from a satisfied client, except perhaps a referral from a satisfied client. If you desire to create the symphonic music of referrals from your clients, you need to have the synchronized efforts of your mortgage partner.

Here are the five steps to protect your client when working with a mortgage originator:

1. Select your mortgage partner well. In every marketplace you will be able to form a partnership with many different mortgage originators. Make sure the partner you are pursuing can add true value to you and your staff. I recommend selecting one mortgage partner and sending business to that individual exclusively. You need to define clearly the criteria under which you will do business. I have seen enormous conflicts between real estate agents and mortgage partners because of differences in business philosophy.

I recommend selecting one mortgage partner and sending business to that individual exclusively.

You both need to understand clearly the philosophy of each other's business.

How often do you both expect to be updated and in what form?

To whom do the updates go, to the agent or to the staff?

What happens in a crisis situation and whom do you call?

What does the mortgage originator have authority to handle on his own?

There is nothing worse for a real estate partner than to be blasted by a client without being warned by the mortgage partner. If you operate your business at a waltz tempo and your mortgage partner is dancing to a polka, that spells trouble. You and your mortgage partner need to be reading from the same sheet of music.

2. Understand how mortgage partners run their business. Some mortgage originators move from one crisis to the next. If the mortgage originator practices this type of crisis management, it will affect your business. You will get clients who expect crisis management to be the norm. Their emotional ups and downs will be greater and more pronounced.

The crisis mode will also affect the quality of the clients mortgage originators refer to you. You cannot allow people who are constantly in crisis mode to enter your business with regularity. Ultimately you will lose control of your business. The value your mortgage partners place on their time will also reflect on you. If they are not prudent with their time, they certainly won't be with yours and they won't teach clients the value of your time. Do you want clients who do not understand your value?

Don't Be Like Lucy and Ethel

Many mortgage originators have haphazard systems. The process is not well defined from the moment a lead is generated until the close. Many mortgage originators have conveyer belt systems that look like an episode of the *I Love Lucy* show. Remember the episode in which Lucy and Ethel are working in a candy factory trying to box chocolates? The conveyer belt speeds up, and Lucy and Ethel can't keep up with the increased production. At first the chocolates drop off the belt. Then the women begin to eat the chocolates to try to keep up. Many mortgage originators run their businesses much like this episode. Poorly organized mortgage originators eat your current income and your past clients. They are eating your future income. They are eating your referral base. As hard as you work to generate a client you can ill afford to lose them at the end of the transaction. If your mortgage partners do not have a solid system, I guarantee they are eating your past clients and future business.

How well does your mortgage originator qualify prospects? You can work only with mortgage originators who control their clients. Any person you allow to become a mortgage partner will have some control over your business because of the clients she refers to you and the systems she has in place to run her business. Make sure your mortgage partner has the ability to control her clients because if she cannot control her clients, neither will you.

Be Part of a Team

The goal is to create strategic partnerships with your affiliates and to help them increase their business, income, and market share. They must also share the same desire for you. The old days, where the agent was the uncompensated and unappreciated sales staff for the lender, title, and escrow industry, are over. We all need to raise our level of service to each other a notch or two. We all have to play together in harmony to achieve longtime clients and profitability. It is in all our best interests to work as a team so that we all can win.

Remember, mortgage originators sometimes make the first impression, and therefore they can set the tone for the transaction.

3. Expect mortgage partners to send you some business. You need to set a standard for the business the mortgage originator sends your way. This standard can be set by the number of transactions or in revenue dollars or both. The days of a mortgage partner saying, "Send me the deal and I will close it," are gone. As agents, we should require our partners to participate in the creation of our success. Your mortgage partner should be committed to helping you achieve your goals. He should account for some of the revenue generated in your business.

4. Make sure your mortgage partner's conveyer belt is solid. Your business is intertwined with your mortgage partners. If they have weak systems, your clients will know it. Weak systems also cause more strain emotionally for agents, lenders, and clients. If your partners do not have a solid system, or conveyer belt, for their business, you will be adversely affected. Either you will need to help them yourself or find someone to help them construct and manage their system properly.

5. Make sure your partners are committed to improvement and change. We all need to be changing and growing. The competition will leave us behind if we don't. Your partners must be working to stay on the cutting edge of the mortgage business. If your partners are not willing to change and grow, search for new partners. The changes in our industry will only accelerate as we move forward. We have seen tremendous growth in technology in the last three to four years. Your partners need to embrace the technology revolution.

Working daily on your education will cause you to stay ahead of your competition and enable you to enjoy life at a greater level.

Create a Mastermind Alliance

You need to have what Napoleon Hill used to call a "mastermind alliance." According to Hill, a mastermind alliance is a "coordination of knowledge and effort, in a spirit of harmony, between two or more people, for the attainment of a definite purpose." Having at least another person that you can labor with and problem-solve with is essential. You can create a frenzy of ideas and excitement by working in concert with another like-minded person whose desire is mutually beneficial. Everyone needs a few good mastermind alliances. I have a few such partners. I have learned a tremendous amount from my mastermind alliances. We all have a strong focus to improve ourselves daily. When we get together we all know we will learn. Your partner needs to be committed to being a lifelong learner.

You and your partners must commit to being lifelong learners. Time dedicated to self-education has to be a scheduled daily activity. Your formal education will allow you to make a living. Your personal or self-education will position you to make a fortune. Becoming highly self-educated will allow you to craft a lifestyle of your dreams. Working daily on your education will cause you to stay ahead of your competition and enable you to enjoy life at a greater level.

Your mortgage partners need to have the same commitment to educating themselves. If they do not, you will leave them behind.

Orchestrate Your Closings

The true goal is to make beautiful music for your clients by putting a smooth, professional, and unemotional closing together. Success starts with the proper selection of the instruments and the players. You must be sure everyone is reading from the same set of sheet music. Of course, you need to make sure your partner is as committed to practicing as you are. Lastly, remember you are the conductor. Ultimately you are responsible for how the music is played. You know what the music should sound like. Do not compromise. If you do, you will have a hard time getting the concert hall filled in the future. Finally, we are all looking for an encore. The encore makes the growth in your career easier. The goal is to create clients that are so happy that they send you referrals.

Build Respect and Recognition

Building a bridge to the other agents in your office and the co-op agents in your marketplace takes time. You will not get recognized overnight. It will take you a number of years to earn the respect and recognition that you desire. Consistently attend events put on by the board and work cooperatively with other agents. Don't be affected by the negative talk of other agents. Stick to building the key relationships that will impact your business and life.

Choose the Company You Keep

Successful people spend time with only four groups of people:

> people they can learn from
>
> people they can have fun with
>
> people they can make money with
>
> people they can teach

Spend your time with only these four groups and you will be on your way to the top.

Developing Relationships with Clients

One of the most difficult challenges for you as a new agent is to create a client relationship with prospects, convincing them that you are the answer to their problems. You don't yet possess the confidence or skill to convert the best prospects all the time. In this chapter we take a look at the different types of clients you will encounter and consider the importance of good communication in nurturing the client-agent relationship.

The way to end up with wonderful clients and satisfied clients is to select them correctly in the first place.

Select the Right Clients

The most important element in creating a solid client relationship is selecting the right client in the first place. I believe that selecting the right client leads to greater success. Too often we work with people

Know When to Walk Away

The path to failure is trying to please everyone with whom you come in contact. When I was in sales, my belief was that I was not put on this earth to help everyone buy and sell. I could not help everyone who showed up. By excluding people, I was able to define and develop better, more loyal clients.

Many of the people we meet are unreasonable and should not be anyone's clients. They become a burden on any agent's time and attention. Our job is to recognize the low probability of their ever becoming a quality client and to take the necessary action of declining to work with them. What a great feeling to be courageous enough to walk away from someone who would otherwise cause my staff and me great frustration. Few agents ever experience the joy of doing business on their own terms, because they compromise their philosophy and belief system for dollars.

who don't have enough desire or motivation for us to do business with them. As a new agent, you are tempted to work with any warm body that is on the phone. (Many agents' idea of a lead is a human being who creates condensation on a piece of glass when held close to his mouth.) However, the way to end up with wonderful clients and satisfied clients is to select them correctly in the first place.

The Four Types of Clients

Here are four different categories of clients with whom you will find yourself working on a regular basis:

Terrific Clients

Most salespeople are just looking for the sale. A professional salesperson is always on the lookout for terrific clients. Terrific clients:

- respect people who are highly skilled at their profession
- listen to advice and guidance that is presented well and that has supporting documentation
- open up about their goals and desires for real estate and their expectation for service

You will always know where terrific clients stand; they don't play "hide the ball." You are not the enemy. You and the terrific clients will be on the same team, working toward a common goal. They also will be fantastic referral sources for your business.

The Magical Sixth Sense of Truth

As a new agent one disadvantage you have is that you have not yet developed the magical sixth sense of truth. Your sixth sense of truth is activated when prospects are not being honest with you, when they don't fully disclose their "hang ups" in selling their home. They hesitate when you ask them if they are working with another agent. You sense that they have not disclosed the extent of their financial picture and find out later there was a bankruptcy two years ago.

No-Clue Clients

No-clue clients live in a dream world. It is difficult to get them to look at the facts and figures that might upset the fantasy world in which they live. These clients really don't want to know the truth that their homes are worth 15 percent less than they think. Each one believes that she will land the one buyer who will pay dramatically above fair market value. Unless the no-clue client has an extremely high motivation, such as a job transfer, divorce, or new children, you will have no sale. If the bottom line is that they *have to* move, you may be able to bring them to reality. In that case, the no-clue client could eventually make progress toward becoming the terrific client.

Unless the no-clue client has an extremely high motivation, such as a job transfer, divorce, or new children, you will have no sale.

Information-Only Clients

These people just want information and expertise from you. They have no intention of creating a relationship of trust; you are there only to provide your knowledge. The information-only client truly believes this approach is justified. He also believes that if you are foolish enough to give your knowledge for free, that's your problem. These clients will take your knowledge and either use it to buy or sell on their own or give it to a friend or family member who doesn't have your skill level and put the business into that person's hands.

Information-only clients will rarely answer direct questions. They are evasive and will challenge your knowledge, beliefs, advice, fees, and services. Ultimately, these challenges will become their justification for not working with you. Sometimes they get offended at your questions. Their belief is that the expertise they can get out of you is useful, but their way is better.

Distrust-Everyone Clients

These clients believe:

- everyone is out to get them
- everyone is trying to reach into their back pockets
- every question you ask comes with its own hidden agenda
- what you are really looking for is the weak point that will allow you to destroy them

Even when, with a lot of care and attention, you manage to win these people over, if you or your team makes one honest error, these clients will be gone. This occurs because they believe that all their negative experiences are just part of a big conspiracy against them.

The Law of Attraction

The Law of Attraction states that we will attract what we are looking for or we will attract what we become. "Like will attract like." I used this law in making decisions regularly with regard to clients. It kept me out of many potential problem-client situations.

Stop the Flow of Problem Clients

Clients who are disrespectful and uncooperative will refer people like themselves to you. I believe people socialize with people like themselves. This type of person stretches your patience and puts a damper on your passion for this career. Do you honestly want more of this type of client? Stop the flow of problem clients. Resolve right

Work Only with Terrific Clients

Selecting and excluding people at the outset is the best way to ensure good client relations. Many problems with clients are caused not by external events or by deficiencies in our interpersonal skills but by the perceptions and expectations of the clients themselves. Some people just don't make good clients.

Create a strong interview process so that you can quickly and efficiently remove the problem prospects before they get inside your inner circle. The price you pay for letting them inside is wasted time, wasted energy, emotional drain, and certainly loss of revenue for you. Focus on working only with terrific clients. You'll be amazed at the increased income and job satisfaction you will enjoy.

High-Maintenance Clients

Problem clients remind me of the scene in the great Billy Crystal–Meg Ryan movie *When Harry Met Sally*. They are at dinner and Billy says to Meg, "You are the worst type of woman. You are a high-maintenance woman who actually thinks she is low maintenance." Many of your clients, if not screened properly, will be like the female character in the movie. They will be high maintenance when they think they are low maintenance.

now to turn down all clients who demand high effort and energy to maintain.

"Being There"

There is one myth we need to address about clients and prospects and our service as real estate agents. For 30 years we have been taught that as real estate agents we must be there for our clients. I hear that all the time from agents across North America, "I want to be there for my clients." What does "be there" mean? Does "be there" mean we are available 24 hours a day, 7 days a week? Does it mean that we miss soccer games, tee ball games, or piano recitals? For many agents that is exactly what it means.

Many of us equate access with service. We have been trained for years that access is the primary vehicle of customer service. We feel we need to be there for our clients. We grant them access to our lives whenever they want it. They can, and will, take over our business, and our lives, if we let them.

Separate Access from Customer Service

I want to share with you a new concept: *Access has nothing to do with customer service*. There are many professionals we do business with who are less than accessible. A skilled doctor cannot be contacted via phone and certainly will not respond within minutes. A skilled doctor is busy with other patients and will get back to the caller during the course of the day. A professional attorney may be in court, in conference, or taking a deposition. When you need to contact them, we don't expect them to return our call immediately. I would certainly question the ability of either of these two professionals if either got back to me right away. Why is it that being phone-available is like a badge of honor for a real estate agent?

Pushing the Wheelbarrow

Ben Franklin said, "If you want a job done right, ask a busy man to do it." Mr. Franklin understood the perception of industrious diligence. He also understood human nature. When Ben Franklin was a young printer he was seen daily on Market Street at noon pushing a wheelbarrow stacked with reams of paper. After becoming successful he confessed that the paper was not in the wheelbarrow because it needed to go somewhere, it was there to promote Ben as a busy man. He created a public perception of value through his daily wheelbarrow walk!

If we choose to meet with clients at all hours of the day and night, they begin to wonder if we have any other clients. We are not promoting being a busy real estate agent. We are promoting that we are not busy and skillful. In order to clearly separate access from customer service, here are a few steps:

Strategy 1: Set Boundaries

Your clients will respect you if you set specific boundaries. Set boundaries on your time away from selling real estate—your personal time. Take out the days off, the family activities, the time with your spouse, and the time for you. Do that before the week begins. The most effective way to lay out boundaries is to execute a set schedule. A set schedule allows you to make each week exactly the same as the week before.

Create specific boundaries by taking your home phone number off your business card. Professionals in other disciplines seldom give out their home number. Turn your cell phone and pager off at specific times each evening.

Strategy 2: Treat Everything As an Appointment

Once you have set boundaries, establish the goal of treating everything as an appointment. Quality time with your family is the most important appointment you have. Don't infringe on this important time. Finally, don't break appointments such as exercising, reading, and relaxing.

You also have appointments in your workday. You have appointments to prospect and to follow up on leads. These time slots will have a tendency to get pushed out of the way by clients. If you allow that to happen, you will see a drop in business within 90 days, when you have no closings. It's easy to let other things take precedence over those prospecting and lead follow-up appointments, but you must overcome the urge to take care of clients in those times.

Strategy 3: Set Specific Times to Return Calls

Many of the calls we get are just not that critical. Clients are trying to give us information they deem as urgent. These calls are rarely emergencies and seldom must be handled right now. Most calls can wait a few hours to address. Set specific times when you return calls, say, once in the late morning and again toward the end of the day. Let people know that you are in appointments and you will be retuning calls at specific times.

Set specific times when you return calls, say, once in the late morning and again toward the end of the day.

Provide Value for Your Client

Now that we have examined a few myths about customers and customer service, we need to look at what to do to provide value for your prospects and clients. Value is created by establishing and maintaining good communication with your buyer or seller and by developing good questioning skills.

Limit Instant Access

You need to separate the concept of access from customer service. Customer service is about getting the job done well. Although your client would prefer total immediate access, they will, in the final analysis, remember your professionalism. Become respected like your doctor, dentist, or attorney. Limit the instant access you grant to people. Don't be fooled by the old access model of total customer service for real estate. To stay competitive with all the changes in the real estate industry, you need to raise the bar on service and professionalism. Access is not in either of these categories.

Effective Communication

One of the key elements of keeping a good prospect or client is effective and consistent communication.

Most of your clients could accept a few reasons for the home not selling. What is unforgivable is silence . . . on your part. Most listing agents become embarrassed or disappointed that the listing has not sold after several weeks so they stop all regular contact with their client. They are afraid of confrontation or a few tough questions, so they have no conversation at all. When a home is on the market for a long time, the worst remedy is no communication.

When to Communicate with Sellers

Sellers that you represent should be called weekly. Select a set time each week when you will call all your sellers. Our time was Friday

What You Don't Know Can't Convince You

The value of good communication cannot be stressed enough. We might have to convince the seller she is overpriced and that a price reduction should be considered. But, if we just show up one day after no contact for 30 days and talk price reduction, we will rarely achieve a lowered price. The reason homes don't sell for months on end is always the price; an adjusted price will usually fix whatever ails the transaction. If we don't communicate this basic fact of real estate to the seller, she will have no reason to understand the importance of a price reduction.

afternoon between 2:30 and 3:30 P.M. This way sellers know exactly when you are going to call. If they are not home, leave an encouraging and informative message.

The key is to update sellers on the activity of their property. Here is what to share with them:

1. Market activity for the week: Indicate the number of homes that went pending in their area at their price range. This will help you in achieving price reductions later on.

2. Your office activity and your activity: This confirms that they made the right selection of agent and company. It also shows there is activity in the marketplace.

3. Specific efforts you made to get their home sold:

- Did you show it?
- What ads ran for the property?
- What type of prospecting and how much prospecting did you do to generate new clients?
- Did you do a broker open house and how many people came?
- Was there any interest in showing it by other agents?
- How many buyer calls did you receive on the property?

4. The marketing plan for next week: Most sellers want to know what to expect from you.

> # "They pounded a sign in the yard and I never heard from them again."
>
>
>
> As a specialist for years in selling expired listings, I got an earful at most listing presentations about the communication from the previous agent. Expired listings are properties that were listed with another agent or broker. Property listings are signed for a specific term and when that term is complete and the property isn't sold, the listings are deemed expired. Lack of communication was the biggest complaint from the seller whose listing had expired. It wasn't that the home did not sell, it was the quality and quantity of the communication. I heard hundreds of times, "They pounded a sign in the yard and I never heard from them again."

5. The feedback from the showings: One of the reasons we did updates to our sellers toward the end of the week was that it allowed us a couple of days to collect feedback from the agents who showed the property. There is an element of excitement for the seller when he comes home and a business card is sitting on the kitchen table. This business card from another agent alerts you that a showing was completed. The seller immediately wants to know if the prospective buyer liked the home.

We always tried to get feedback from other agents to share with our seller. This also enabled us to have a few extra sets of eyes with regard to the property's condition and price. We used the other agents' evaluations to help us retrieve future price reductions if required.

By contacting your sellers weekly, you increase the level of respect and trust they have for you. You will avoid the biggest frustration for your sellers—lack of communication.

When to Communicate with Buyers

Buyer clients have communication needs as well. Regular contact with a highly motivated buyer builds trust. A buyer who is looking to purchase now needs a lot of communication, care, and attention. There is no such thing as too much communication for this type of buyer. You can't call them frequently enough. When a buyer is extremely anxious to purchase a home, call her every day. Call her just to say, "I have looked on the hot sheet of new homes on the market today twice. There are no new properties that meet your criteria. Let's hope that tomorrow there will be something new. Thanks for the opportunity to serve you. Have a great day."

A buyer who is looking to purchase now needs a lot of communication, care, and attention. There is no such thing as too much communication for this type of buyer.

This approach repeated day after day will let your buyers know that nothing will get by you. Demonstrate that you are an expert and a professional and they will come to know that they hired the right person to represent them. You will not receive that call from the buyer to tell you she found another house over the weekend at an open house and purchased it from the agent that was holding it. That is one of the most gut-wrenching calls an agent can receive. All that time, effort, and energy you invested to earn a commission has vaporized. Constant and consistent communication is the best insurance policy against that painful experience.

Communication During Escrow

Your communication doesn't stop after you sell a house, whether it was your listing or not. Once you accomplish that goal you must still communicate with the client weekly through the escrow process. To help you develop a long-term client relationship, your communication should be ongoing and helpful.

During this period there are inspections, repairs, and appraisals of the home for value, and often title challenges or even loan problems. Our job is to communicate fully with all parties in every transaction that we represent. In addition, we have a responsibility to communicate with the other parties who facilitate the transaction, such as the other agent, title company representative, loan officer, attorneys, appraisers, home inspectors, and repair contractors.

Happy Clients Generate Referrals

The goal for anyone in a sales profession is to generate referrals from their clients. Those referrals are the evidence that the job was done professionally. They also provide an excellent source of revenue to your business long term. Remember that it costs 10 times as much to find a new client than to retain the client with whom you already have done business. Communication is a huge factor in retention.

Communicate After Closing

Most agents rarely call their clients after the transaction closes. The National Association of Realtors did a study recently. They interviewed home buyers and sellers and found out 80 percent of the consumers never went back to their original agent for one reason . . . The agent never called them again. Now isn't that fascinating? As a new agent who is going to be a professional and call your clients regularly, you have a tremendous opportunity. You can retain your clients and acquire the clients of many other agents because those agents are not going to be doing what you will do.

Communication After Transfer of Title

Let me outline a plan that will connect you with your clients for life. The mainstay of the plan is personal contact with the client. This plan starts right after the close and transfer of title.

1. You call your client one day after the closing and thank her for the opportunity to serve her. Ask if there is anything she needs from you.

2. Call her the fifth day after closing and see how the move went. Did she live through the process? How is she settling in? Did she find anything not quite right with the home that she needs your assistance to solve? Thank her again for the opportunity to serve her. Then ask her for referrals. Here is a great script:

> Betty, I am sure all your friends and coworkers are every excited about your move into your new home. In your conversations has anyone mentioned wanting to make a move like you have just done? Please keep me in mind when they do. My business is built on referrals from great clients like you.

3. Repeat this process about 2 weeks after the close and 30 days after the property closes. By continuing to communicate after closing, you are adding value. Great salespeople are always adding more value than they receive in income from a sales transaction. In the client's mind the sale was made weeks ago and your compensation happened then. He is amazed that you would call after you got paid to see how he is doing. The more you follow up after the close, the more likely that client separates you from the commission.

Express Your Concern

Imagine how you would feel if that salesperson who sold you the new car called you in a week to see if you were enjoying it! You would feel totally different about that salesperson. You would say, "He got paid for the sale, but he is still calling to check on me. He is really concerned about me. He is more focused on my satisfaction than the money." Your clients will feel the same way about you when you call after the close.

Don't Forget Past Clients

A great salesperson is never done providing service and value to his customers. You want to continue this process of follow-up at least twice a year for the rest of your career. Don't make the mistake that many agents make early in their career and not call your past clients. I meet agents daily that are 5, 10, even 20 years in the business who are not doing this simple past client follow-up. They have to go out and find new clients daily because they did not care for their past clients. It's like the rancher who continues to bring cattle into the barn but never checks to close the back door of the barn. He will always have to bring in more cattle to feed his family. Don't make the error that most agents make. Start to follow up and build that solid relationship with your past clients today.

Develop Your Questioning Skills

The last essential skill in developing strong relationships with your clients is the ability to ask probing questions. The best way to build trust and be recognized as the expert is to ask questions. Highly skilled salespeople understand the power of questions.

The questions you ask lead to or away from the sale. For too long we have been led to believe that highly successful salespeople are fast-talking motor-mouths who can talk someone into buying. "Gary is such a great talker he could sell a refrigerator to an Eskimo." A great salesperson, however, will question the client or prospect completely and realize that an Eskimo has no need to purchase that refrigerator—a space heater might be something she really needs.

The best way to build trust and be recognized as the expert is to ask questions.

As a future top-gun agent, your ability to question your prospects and clients will enable you to help them achieve their objectives. You will not be able to help them achieve their goals if you don't know what those goals are.

Some key questions that are often overlooked by agents are:

Why are you moving?

What are you trying to accomplish by moving?

Where are you hoping to move to?

How soon do you want to be in your new home?

Describe for me the home you want to live in?

Ultimately, what will a move into the home you described do for your family?

The last question is significant because in the answer you will find the feeling, emotion, or value your clients attach to the move. You may discover the driving passion underlying why they are making a decision to move. With an understanding of that feeling, you will be able to help your clients meet their objective.

Go for First Place

Building strong relationships with clients and prospects will increase the speed at which you reach the top in real estate sales. Having the mindset to play for first place, never settling for second, will help you avoid many of the frustrations in working on 100 percent commission.

Finding Mentors

According to Webster's dictionary, a mentor is a "guide or trusted counselor or teacher." You can have mentors for different areas of your life. You could have a mentor for your health, for your business, or for your spiritual life.

Mentors help you define your philosophy of life, develop your skills, and lay out a plan for you. An effective mentor should be an outstanding role model whose lead and guidance you are honored to follow. She should be someone you envision being like in the future. A true mentor is there to come alongside you and show you the ropes, helping you formulate your goals and assisting you in your plan to achieve those goals. She is also there to correct you when you have taken a wrong turn and to map out for you a more effective approach.

An effective mentor should be an outstanding role model whose lead and guidance you are honored to follow.

99

Avoid Choosing a Mentor on the Basis of "the Show"

One of the most challenging steps for a new agent to take is the selection of the right mentor. Too often you can be lured into believing a particular person would be a quality mentor and later discover, with great disappointment, it was a mistake. As a new agent, you can easily be influenced by someone who appears to be an expert or "top gun" agent. We see the agents who drive expensive cars and live in big houses and conclude that we want to be just like them. In many cases you would feel differently if you knew the whole truth. Some of these agents are paying an incredible price to live "the show" and often spend too much time at work, investing very little in their family or spouse. They may be in debt up to their eyeballs to keep "the show" going. As they often say in Texas, "Big hat, no cattle." There can be a lot of show with little substance behind it.

The Myth of Sales Volume

As agents, we become caught up in the myth of sales volume. Belief in this myth causes some of the greatest damage in this industry. Do not be fooled by the sales volume myth. More agents have gone down in flames chasing their sales volume than from any other myth in real estate.

We glorify the agents with high sales volume and promote and encourage other agents to be more like them. We award agents and offices based on sales volume, with little regard to the other factors that make up success in careers and lives. New agents look on in reverence, thinking the person who has the most production in sales volume is the example to follow. I would like to take an objective look at the true value of sales volume and point out some other factors to keep in mind when evaluating your business and other agents when considering a mentor. These are also questions you will need to answer about your own business someday.

We need to see beyond "the show" to the real truth. I believe that ultimately character counts far more then the plaques and awards. When we strip everything away, it is not about the plaque. We don't want to end up saying, "I ran the race, I got the T-shirt, what's next?" Let's take a look at six important questions. I believe you will come away with a different perspective on sales volume.

Consider These Questions When Selecting a Mentor

1. Is the better salesperson the one with more sales volume or the one with more sale units sold and closed?
2. When does profitability enter into the picture and does it have any importance?
3. Should the amount of time actually worked be considered when evaluating an agent's ability?
4. What is the true quality of life for the agent, in terms of health, time worked, time off, stress, and so on?
5. How does the quality of service delivered to clients factor in?
6. Are you taking steps to achieve financial independence based on your own definition of success?

Is the Better Salesperson the One with the Higher Sales Volume or the One with More Sale Units Sold and Closed?

Clearly they both possess merit for what they do. However, we know historically that the one with the highest sales volume is traditionally placed on a pedestal, while the one with the most units sold is placed only halfway up.

In some cases, sales volume can reflect the value of the market, not the value of the agent. For example, one agent's average price range is $100,000, so his average commission check is $3,000. This agent closes 65 deals a year and earns a gross commission of $195,000. Across town there is another agent with an average price of homes sold of $300,000 and an average commission check amounting to $9,000. This agent closes 25 transactions a year and earns a gross commission of $225,000. Who has more options in his business and just may be a better salesperson?

I think there are strengths to both. The agent who does 65 deals only needs to raise his sales price because he already demonstrated that he is able to achieve 65 closed sales per year. He understands the process and if he has set up his business properly; he only needs to apply his philosophy of business in a higher sales price range to earn more income. He also did almost three times as many transactions.

Usually the agent with the higher average commission receives all the rewards from peers, brokers, owners, and the company. The second agent is held in high esteem because he was the high producer in the office. This agent has a good business but sold only two homes per month (by most sales standards this is not earth-shattering). This agent needs to learn how to close more transactions to increase his business. Which one really has a business that is poised to go to the next level?

When Does Profitability Enter into the Picture and Does It Have Any Importance?

In my career of selling real estate, coaching, and speaking, I have met many agents who are making a very high gross income, but have little net income.

Every New Idea Must Pay for Itself

Some agents invest all their income back into their business in the form of gimmicks, marketing, gifts, mailings, advertising, and over-paying staff. They make decisions based on the idea that if they get one more transaction per month it will pay for this new gimmick. The unfortunate thing is that they evaluate many parts of their business this same way. Suddenly they need nearly all they make monthly just to cover these gimmicks. Every new idea must pay for itself as well as generate a satisfactory profit. I expected at least a ten-fold return for any investment. If I spent $1,000 on a new idea, I planned to receive $10,000 in return from it.

The Real Cost of a Promotional Idea

Most agents do not factor their time, or the staff's time, into the cost of a new idea. That is a legitimate cost that must be included. For example, the cost to mail something is not just the cost of the stamp. It's the cost of the letterhead, envelope, stamp, label, staff time to prepare it, and your time to oversee the process. That's the overall cost and you should demand a tenfold return.

The best mentors understand the profit formula in real estate. They clearly watch and evaluate the cost of their business.

You must evaluate each program so that you remain profitable. We all work too hard to earn wages without profits. The best mentors understand the profit formula in real estate. They clearly watch and evaluate the cost of their business. This mentor will be of great value to your career.

Profits Go Farther Than Wages

Many agents have bought themselves a job and never make a profit. A wise man once said, "Profits are better than wages." Profits are the dollars you have left after you pay your wages and all your bills.

Profits, when invested, beget more profits, creating financial independence. Wages merely cover the monthly bills.

Agents need to view the whole picture: the gross and the net. To find the best measure of your profitability after all the hype of sales volume, gross commission earned, and all the other ego-stroking we do, look at line 32 on your federal tax return. That is where you come face to face with reality—what you truly made for all your efforts last year. Do not kid yourself! Too often agents talk about what they grossed in income. You will hear the term GCI, or gross commission income. That term means only what you brought in, not what you net—get to live on, invest, and spend. Don't get faked out so easily! What you are taxed on is what you really made. What you really made is after your expenses.

Should the Amount of Time Actually Worked Be Considered When Evaluating an Agent's Ability?

I know many agents who work six to seven days a week in order to generate their income. If they factored in the actual time worked versus what they earned, they would feel sick, because their actual per-hour wage is so disappointing. In fact, if you asked them if they would do what they do for that hourly wage, they would say, "No."

If you want a dose of reality, divide your hours worked into line 32 on your federal income tax form. That is what you truly made per hour. That is what you would earn if you were an employee. For some agents, this exercise is too scary to even imagine. But you may want to ask yourself this tough question . . . Do you want to make that again this year?

Work Less, Do More

We all can do more in less time. In my fourth year of real estate sales, I switched to a four-day workweek, Monday through Thursday. My production increased more than 30 percent each successive year. I reduced my time working by at least one full day while showing increases in after-tax earnings. My skills improved exponentially, and my focus and concentration intensified. I also reclaimed my life for my family and myself. I was able to spend three days a week with my family. I also increased my time investment in personal development, which leads me to the next question:

What Is the True Quality of Life for the Agent in Terms of Health, Time Worked, Time Off, Stress, and So On?

You cannot be a 7-days-a-week wonder forever. At some point you need to reclaim your life. You have to control your clients and the other agents. My philosophy is that earning large sums of money is the easiest area of your life to improve. However, working to improve your spiritual, mental, physical, family, and financial areas is far more challenging.

Give Your Time Off the Same Value As Your Work Time

When you schedule your time off and place the same value on it as you do your work time, you will have the opportunity to reclaim your life. Your productivity will increase dramatically during your work

> *The value of my time with my family is worth more than my work time.*

time. The value of my time with my family is worth more than my work time. If you have that philosophy, you will focus on your family when away from work and focus on work when at work. While many agents are at work, they think they should be at home. When they are at home, they are mentally reviewing their work rather than focusing on their spouse and children. Wherever you are, be there!

How Does Quality of Service Delivered to Clients Factor In?

To create a sustainable business you need to take care of your clients. The agent who continually works with new clients and rarely gets referrals or repeat business is lacking in service. Although we all need to spend some of our day finding new clients, realize that long-term success comes from repeat and referral business from clients who are already sold on our service. Are you doing the job you were hired to do? Do you provide the best service you can in your present marketplace?

The Product You Are Selling Is Yourself

Part of providing better customer service is improving your product. The product you are selling is first and foremost yourself. If you are not spending significant amounts of time improving yourself, your competitors will eventually pass you. Jim Rohn reminds us that you need to work as hard on yourself as you do on your job. Following this advice will lead you to both personal and professional greatness. If you are not investing at least a half an hour a day in personal development, you will be left behind.

Spend Time Investing in Yourself

When I entered real estate sales in 1990, I started in a very successful office where all the agents were veterans of 10 years and more. Most of the agents were not spending time in personal development of their own lives. This resulted in my being the top agent in the office by my third year in the business. In another short period of time I was in the top 10 in a four-state region of over 1400 agents.

I share this not to brag, but to encourage. If you spend the time to invest in yourself you will achieve the same results. Your personal education will have as much to do with your future success as anything else you do. My biggest challenge in life is getting the hours that I need daily in personal development to stay ahead of my coaches, my clients, and the real estate community. Your mentor also has to be focused on personal growth.

Great mentors will always be spending time in personal development. They will allot time weekly to improving themselves. This type of a mentor will be able to help you long term. A mentor who does not want to improve will be of little value after a few years and in that situation the master will, in the near future, become the student.

Are You Taking Steps to Achieve Financial Independence Based on Your Own Definition of Success?

Everyone has her own definition of what constitutes financial independence. Take the time to clearly define yours. Plan how you are going to get from where you are today to where you want to be. Your mentor can help you with your plan, but make sure your mentor has a plan as well. Unfortunately, too many people fail to plan their future.

Include Savings in Your Plan

Often the agents with the highest gross commission save and invest little or no money. They believe there is always tomorrow, and if they could just earn more they could then save more, but they have no plan for how they will do that. We often spend to make up for shortcomings in our unbalanced lives. We need to create a plan that includes savings so we can achieve financial independence.

Develop the discipline to save right now, today. Saving does not get easier when the numbers get bigger. Instead, the want list gets longer because you think you deserve it and can afford it. Only you control the destiny of your money. You must create that savings plan today.

Financial Independence Is a Measure of Success

Our goal in life should be to be financially independent. We should all have the desire to amass enough assets to retire comfortably by living off the income or interest they generate. When we get the financial issue out of the way, we can really begin to live life to the fullest.

Financial independence is the true measure of success in the real estate business. In fact, it is the measure of success in any business. Why should we as real estate agents be any different?

Selecting the Right Mentor

The ideal mentor possesses all of the qualities we have been discussing. If you cannot find one person who has them all, select several mentors who, combined, possess all the guidance you need.

Look for a person who is several levels above your present situation. The biggest producer in the company, for example, may be exciting, but could be a very poor choice. Often, these individuals have been at the top so long they have forgotten how they did it. The game of real estate sales may have changed since they where climbing the ladder. On the other hand, if you identify a person just a few levels above you, you are more apt to find a more relevant and helpful mentor. You also want to select someone who is growing, not stagnant. If you determine that he is not growing, you will have to change mentors in the near future.

You want to select someone who is growing, not stagnant.

Questions to Ask a Mentor

When you approach people about being your mentor, ask them some key questions:

1. What are the essential skills to achieve peak performance in real estate sales?

This question will assess prospective mentors' knowledge of real estate sales. The key word is *skills*. Many agents you ask will not mention true skills such as prospecting, knowing your scripts, effective lead follow-up techniques, managing the revenue, and controlling expense. You will hear answers as superficial as: You have to like being around people; you have to be available for your clients to service them. These are not skills, they are feelings and you can't build replication and increased revenue in your business based on feelings.

2. What are some of the obstacles I am going to face?

These obstacles need to be identified and defined in order for you to be prepared to face them. A good follow-up question here would be, "What could I specifically learn about obstacles from your experience in real estate sales?"

3. What resources are available that will better ensure my growth and success?

Your prospective mentor should be able to tell you about specific classes, tapes, books, scripts, and coaching.

4. What expertise did you have from your past that helped you develop the skill to excel?

5. How did you decide to enter real estate?

At this point they might share with you a little of their personal history and philosophy regarding real estate sales. This will allow you to gauge the depth of their success in life.

6. What are your goals and how do you plan to achieve them?

The answer will tell you how big a thinker they are right now. You always want to hang out with big thinkers because they make you think bigger. Don't spend your time with people who only want to make enough money to buy a new piece of furniture. They may be ahead of you today, but very shortly they will be behind you.

7. How can I help you achieve your goals?

When you ask this question you may get a blank stare because most people have probably never been asked such a question. Remain silent and

Be the Lead Dog

There is an old saying, "The only dog in a dog sled team that gets to see the world is the lead dog." All the others behind the lead dog all have the same view: the others' behinds. You were created to take the lead so you can control your income. Because you are going to have the same view for a while, make sure at least you are moving forward.

wait for their answer. You have to ask this because you will learn more while helping them than you will on your own. The more experience and opportunities you have, the quicker you will learn and grow.

8. Can I share my goals with you?

In order to share your goals, you first need to have some. We are going to teach you in depth how to create solid, compelling goals. Good follow-up questions are:

> What do you think of my goals?
>
> Would you help me achieve them?

These questions will give you feedback about your goals. They will cause the mentor candidates to evaluate their own level of involvement. You will learn right away if they are the right person for you. I would be cautious about those individuals who want to think about it for a week. They either have the desire to do it or they don't. They either have a passion to invest in others or they do not.

How to Ask Someone to Be Your Mentor

Once you have defined and identified a mentor, what is the next step? At this point I would encourage an indirect approach. You don't go up to someone who you have decided would be a great mentor and say, "Here I am." Share with the potential mentor how valuable his advice has been and how much you have already learned. People appreciate hearing that their counsel helped you better define your goals and objectives.

A True Mentor Sees What You Can Become

I speak, write, coach, and create tools like tapes, CDs, and videos not for the money, but for the joy and satisfaction of learning how the lives of others are being changed and improved. A true mentor does it for the satisfaction of seeing another achieve her full potential in life. A truly skilled, caring mentor does not look at you the way you are now. He looks at you the way you will be. I see my coaching clients the way they will be or could be. I see them with their business and life in order. My job as a coach or mentor is to draw for them the exciting picture of what their life will be like in the future. Then, I can help them craft the plan and the steps to achieve and fulfill that vision.

What Mentors Require of You

Many mentors may test you at the very beginning of the relationship. Once someone approached me about mentoring him, but I was not sure if he would be the type of person I could teach to be successful in real estate. In order to test him, I asked him to read two specific books and call me in a week. I thought that would be the end of him. I told him in no uncertain terms that a week meant 7 days, not 8, not 10, but 7. He called me back in a week. He had read the books and asked, "Now, what's next?" Then I had him practice a couple of scripts that he would role-play with me in 5 days. He came back in 5 days and had them down pat. I gave him instructions to listen to two tape series in 5 days and report back to me. He did what he was told and had some of the concepts down from the tapes. This process went on for almost a month. He did everything I asked him to do in the time frame required. At the end of a month he became my mentee. He earned my respect by doing each thing that I asked.

Mentors Look for a Strong Desire to Succeed

Most mentors will expect you to have a strong desire to advance to the top and make the effort to get there. They may send you away as I did to see if your passion will surpass theirs. The mentee has to bring a high level of passion into the relationship. That is the value a mentee brings in. The mentee just discussed ignited a fire in me that burned for some time. He helped me improve my skills along the way. Knowing a skill and being able to teach it are two different things. The benefit for the mentor is a rekindling of the passion for the business and an extra boost from someone young or new in the business.

The Value of Coaching

Coaching is another form of mentoring. Coaching for peak performers has been around for years. For many decades the most successful athletes have been coached to win the big event. Tiger Woods would not be the golfer he is today without his golf coaches. Michael Jordan, John Elway, and Michael Johnson have all had coaches. The leaders of some of the most successful companies in the business world have coaches. Behind each great milestone or accomplishment stand two people—the one who executes the task or carries out the game plan and the one who helps to create the game plan and teaches the executor to improve his skills. Maybe it is time to evaluate and consider the benefits of a coach.

A good coach has five basic traits. When these traits are used to help you move forward in your life, the results are amazing. A coach can help you increase your production and enjoyment in life and help you craft a life of long-term success.

The Ability to Listen

The first trait of a great coach is the ability to listen and help you clarify your goals and vision in all areas of your life. Earl Nightingale, the famous speaker, stated that we are goal-seeking organisms. Our purpose is to set and achieve goals in life. The difficulty for most people is not in trying to achieve their goals, but in setting them in the first place. We can accomplish anything in life provided we truly decide to do it.

The Belief That Goals Must Have Deadlines

The second trait of a successful coach is the understanding that all goals must have deadlines. Deadlines get one's juices and thoughts flowing to create the desired result. Have you ever planned to go away for vacation and two days before you are to leave you go into a flurry of activity in your business? It is because of the deadline that the activity increases and things begin to happen. How would you like to have that kind of production level ongoing? Determine effective deadlines for all areas of your business.

Deadlines get one's juices and thoughts flowing to create the desired result.

The Ability to Create a Game Plan and Execute It

A great coach will take the goals and vision you set for yourself and teach you to achieve them. She will help you create the step-by-step game plan to reach that envisioned future. Even the big projects that seem like mountains can be broken down into bite-size pieces, which are called daily disciplines. A great coach will also show clients the consequences of not following through on their goals and commitments.

The Ability to Motivate and Inspire

The coach will provide ongoing motivation and inspiration during the storms of life. We will experience many storms in this world; we cannot avoid them. Because we cannot avoid them, we must prepare for them. It is not the storm that causes the problem, it is how we react to the storm. A great coach will help you brace for the storm that otherwise might overwhelm you. Coaching provides the motivation and inspiration to overcome life's storms.

The Habit of Accountability

Lastly, a great coach provides accountability and is available for you. A great coach will help you evaluate your progress against your goals and vision. He will hold you to the standard that you have set for yourself.

Feed Yourself Bite-Size Pieces

I had a client in 1998 who wanted to earn more than $250,000 for the year, when the year before he had earned only $130,000. We worked diligently to break down into bite-size pieces what he needed to accomplish in order to achieve his goal. Once the bite-size pieces were determined, we were able to set the daily disciplines for him to undertake. Because he had to focus just on his daily disciplines, the task was not paralyzing. When he got behind in achieving his goal, it was always caused by his not doing his daily disciplines. As his coach I helped him create the game plan and targeted him to execute it daily. He achieved and broke his goal by earning more than $265,000 for 1998, which was more than a 100 percent increase in his business. Coaching really works in real estate sales as in other fields.

The Benefits of Coaching

The truth is that everyone needs a coach. Hiring a coach is making an investment in you. The benefits of coaching produce years of dividends. Where would Michael Jordan be without his coaches? Great coaches enable their clients to increase their abundance more rapidly without experiencing the many mistakes and pitfalls of being on their own. We all have had coaches and teachers throughout our lives. The most successful people never outgrow mentors. They work with coaches to achieve peak performance. Do not neglect to make the investment in yourself for you and your family.

Meeting Challenges

M ost people enter the real estate sales profession without a clear understanding of how to run a business. New agents enter the profession from different backgrounds and professions. The readers of this book may be former homemakers, flight attendants, students, salespeople, or restaurant workers: a true melting pot of professions. But most new agents have never dealt with the issues of running a business; they usually are just beginning or have just finished their classroom training to receive their real estate license.

The Profit Factor

As I have said for years to my audiences and my coaching clients, training has nothing to do with running a profitable business. I have always considered myself a businessperson who happened to sell real estate.

Even a Dentist Must Know How to Run a Business

My father, Norm, was a dentist for 30 years, and he taught me a great deal about how to run a business. A large degree of his success was attributed to two factors: He knew how to run his practice and how to live within his means. I asked him recently what he recalls as the hardest part of starting his dental practice. He didn't hesitate in saying, "Learning to understand and to run my business." Just as in your real estate school training, he was not taught in dental school how to run a business. They taught him the skill of being a dentist— tooth extractions, gold crowns, cleaning, fillings, and drilling. They never taught him the billing part of the business, the part where you collect your money. They also never taught him the value of time.

The purpose of a business is to create and keep customers. When I ask at a seminar, "What is the purpose of a business?" most people answer, "To turn a profit or to make money." Eighty percent of businesses fail because they lack customers or, put another way, ample sales volume. The objective, then, is to service your customers well so you keep them for life. Profit is the natural result of a well-run business. Profit will happen if we create and keep customers and watch expenses. The greatest challenge is to learn to understand and to run your business. This challenge is not unique to real estate.

Time and Profit

The biggest obstacle to success in any profession is getting paid for your time. Real estate school education will not teach you how to be successful. It will not teach you how to run a business. The school will not teach techniques for mastering time. Ultimately, your time is your most precious resource. It is far more valuable than money. Time is ever ticking and advancing. Time is the true asset of life.

The real difficulty is not the lack of time; it is what we do with the time that we have. It is how we control our daily allotment of 24 hours. Actually, we really only have 16 hours to use because we need 8 for sleep and rest. It's what we do in those remaining 16 hours during each day that results in success or creates failure. Because we can never stockpile, accumulate, or turn back time, we have to control the passing of it.

So it comes down to being a matter of learning to do what is most important first each day. When at work we must do what generates the most revenue in the shortest time.

When I am on the road speaking, I see agents daily who earn more money only because they spend more time in their business. Now, anyone can earn more money if she invests more time. Even a ditchdigger can do that by working overtime. But successful people prefer to increase the return on the time they invest.

Mastery of Time Gives Us More Options

Ultimately, it all boils down to what are you worth per hour. This number is critical to know during your entire sales career. You must check this number with regularity to ensure its improvement. By raising your hourly rate, you gain more choices in life. If you were earning $25 an hour selling real estate and you controlled your time better and improved your skills so that just six months later you were earning $50 an hour, you would have options you didn't have before. You could now work fewer hours and make the same amount of money. You could now spend more time with your family. You could also choose to work the same amount of hours, but double your pay. This would allow a better lifestyle, more investments, more savings, and better schools for your children. The combinations and possibilities are endless. You have now created options for yourself and your family. The key to growth and abundance in real estate sales is mastery of time.

The key to growth and abundance in real estate sales is mastery of time.

We Are Selling Our Time

As a real estate agent, there are only two things you are selling. Neither of these assets is houses. You are selling your time first and foremost. Your time is the commodity that's for sale. If it takes you 50 hours to find the buyer a home, you will not get paid the same for your time if it took you only 25 hours for the same task. Because the price for our service from agent to agent is fairly constant, time is the asset we are selling.

We Are Selling Our Knowledge

The other asset we are selling is our knowledge. We control our knowledge by controlling our time. As a new agent, you are going to be selling time more than knowledge because your knowledge has less value today than it will in the future. However, many agents have not increased their knowledge in 20 years, so they still have to sell time. The only way to increase knowledge is to invest time in reading, studying, attending seminars, practicing scripts and dialogues, viewing videotapes, and actually working with buyers and sellers. You must have time to be able to increase the value of your knowledge.

How to Figure Your Value

The more I coach and train agents, the more I realize the biggest battle they have is on the battlefield of time. Maximizing the dollars we earn per hour separates the extremely successful agents from those who are frustrated. Many agents across the country are merely trading more time for more money. They are simply spending more and more time with people other than their family. However, if you know your hourly rate you can change that. Here is how to figure out your value:

To figure out what you make per hour, take your gross commission (that's before company split) and divide it by the number of hours worked. To find hours worked, take the number of hours you work in a day, multiply by the days you work a week and the number of weeks you work per year, then divide that into your gross commission.

Task Analysis

We are all squeezed for time. We all feel there are not enough hours in the day. We all feel the tug between our family and our business and the battle for abundance in both areas. If you truly want to find a few hours daily, try task analysis.

First, find out what it is you actually do each day. Take an old appointment book page and make a few copies. Then every 15 to 30 minutes, write down what you are doing. Do this for two weeks. This process will enable you to know with certainty where you are investing your time.

You will be amazed at the allocation of your time. Most agents who have completed this task find 10 to 20 hours a week that can be better spent. That's anywhere from 25 to 50 percent increased efficiency when fully implemented! To know what that really means to you in dollars,

What Is Worth $50 an Hour?

If you know your value per hour, you will be able to evaluate what you do on the basis of whether or not it really pays you that amount per hour. Let's say you make $50 an hour. There are only certain activities in selling real estate that will pay you that $50 per hour. The rule is if you would not pay someone $50 to do something, neither will anyone else. This means that you will not be earning your $50 an hour doing those activities. For example, making flyers, inputting listings into the multiple listing service, putting together bulk mail, and typing letters are all activities that I would not pay anyone $50 an hour to do. But these have to be done. The question is, are you the person to do them or can you spend less time doing them?

multiply your gross commission by 25 percent. That is what you can earn in addition this year without more expenses, without the latest marketing gimmicks. The best part is that you are in total control of that number. The market, your broker, buyers, and sellers have no effect on your ability to increase your income by the amount you wrote down.

Work diligently on the task analysis process. Really track your activities and the time invested in each. At the end of each week add up the time spent in each activity. Ask yourself these questions:

1. Am I getting paid _____ per hour for each activity?
2. How can I reduce the time I am spending in each activity that pays less than _____?
3. Do I really need to do this activity?
4. Can I get someone else to do this activity?

You Control Your Own Time

Knowing what you are worth per hour and how you are investing your work time are the first two steps to time mastery. Once you have started down the road to time mastery, you are moving toward sales mastery and finally life mastery. Make the commitment today to yourself and your family to do this exercise. The harsh reality of life is—we do not know how long we have to enjoy it. We can make up lost revenue, but we cannot make up lost time. Know that your time is the most valuable resource you have. Start the process to reclaim more of it today.

We can make up lost revenue, but cannot make up lost time. Know that your time is the most valuable resource you have.

We have the ultimate control of our own time. We are the owners of our time and it is our responsibility to control our time. It rests on no one else.

Clients' View of a Real Estate Agent

One challenge of being a real estate agent is that clients don't regard us as professionals, and sometimes even we ourselves don't. If we were playing baseball, we would have three strikes against us before we even got up to bat.

Strike One: Unreasonable Requests from Clients

The general public has little or no respect for us largely because they do not understand what we really do. Most people think that if they call or page us we should return their call within minutes and be ready to drop everything to show them a home or meet with them. They think we should show them our listings at any time of the day or night, even if they have no serious intentions of buying—it may be out of their price range; perhaps they have not met with a lender yet. For example, once I received a call from someone because his agent was out of town and he wanted me to show him a home. This person wanted me to leave my family for one or two hours on the weekend so he could see the home. This potential buyer was never going to buy the home *through me* even if he decided to buy! The odds of his actually purchasing this particular home were maybe 10 to15 percent. Why would I want to break away from my family for one of my listings to sell at that rate? I would not make such a poor decision.

My belief is that I am not obligated to fulfill any such unreasonable requests. I am not obligated to take time away from my family to show potential buyers a house because they want to see it right now. If most people called their doctor and wanted to see her right now,

Respect Your Billable Hours

How many times have you called an attorney to ask a few quick questions and you are billed for 15 to 30 minutes of time? You will receive a statement almost every time. Rarely do attorneys not start the meter when they pick up the phone. They do because the caller is buying their knowledge and their time. Why should we as agents be different? I know I provide as much value as an attorney, do you?

they could not. Why should real estate agents be treated any differently than doctors? If the prospect on the other end of the phone has no respect for your time, he will not have respect for the other aspects of your service as well. He also will not have respect for you as a person. If a prospect has little respect for you, his attitude will not change when he becomes a client.

You must earn a level of respect for your time on the first call, whether you call the prospect or the prospect calls you. You must set the tone that your time is valuable, and if you are going to give the prospect some of your time, expect to be paid—by turning him into a client.

Strike Two: Twenty-Four-Hour Access

We help perpetuate the problem by not controlling access. Too many agents are available 24 hours a day, 7 days per week. There is no other profession whose members are on call 24/7, yet we seem proud that we are there for our clients at all times. Our clients do not work a schedule like that in their job. Take back your family time. Inform your clients of your days and evenings off and stick to your schedule. Do you really want to do business with someone who does not want you to have days off or family time? It is solely up to you to set a clear standard.

Strike Three: Haphazard Work Habits

We are independent contractors. We get to do what we want when we want to do it. I have observed some of the work habits of my colleagues. It is not a mystery to me why many of them do not make any money, and some of these agents have sold real estate for 10 to 20 years. If you want to make any money, you must treat yourself and your career with respect. Show up at the office at the same time every day. Complete your workday at the end of the day. Do not regularly take a two-hour lunch break. Treat this career like a real job or a real career. Your clients are counting on you to do so. If you have that philosophy, you cannot help being successful. I have never seen an agent who came in early and put in a full day's work who was not successful. Remember that no one is going to help you develop the time management disciplines you need but you yourself. Your broker or manager will not be able to magically give you that ability.

There are some specific techniques that will help you achieve more in less time. There are also sales skills that will enable you to produce at a higher level. We will be sharing those in chapter 8. First, we need to reduce the strike count, so you are able to see more pitches to hit. Your second goal is to be a better hitter, whether you are trying to hit for an average and do a lot of transactions or are looking to hit the long ball out of the park with big deals.

Compressing time is the ability to accomplish more in less time. If you analyze the highest producers in business, you will observe they all have this skill.

Compressing Time

One of the skills top achievers have is the ability to compress time. Compressing time is the ability to accomplish more in less time. If you analyze the highest producers in business, you will observe they all have this skill.

Plan for Tomorrow

Plan your work tomorrow before you leave today. If you spend a few minutes planning your day on paper the day before, your subconscious mind will kick in, working on your challenges of the next day while you sleep. Your mind will be working like a rotisserie, turning the challenges and your time for tomorrow all night while you rest. When you get up, you will be ready to attack the day.

Focus Your Day

Before you start your workday make sure to ask these key questions:

1. What is the highest payoff activity I can do?
2. What activity, if done with excellence, can make the biggest difference?
3. What can I do well that no one else can do?
4. Why am I on the payroll?

Do What You Do Best

These questions must be asked each day before you begin. The most successful people don't try to be a jack-of-all-trades. They are the people who specialize in performing activities that no one else can do. They perform these actions with excellence. If you do that you will be highly sought after.

Urgent Versus Important

Successful people understand the trap of *Urgent* versus *Important*. As real estate agents we are faced with that challenge every day. We get interrupted constantly by phone calls that are urgent, not important. We have to make quick judgments on unexpected calls from other agents, sellers, buyers, title companies, and escrow people. The consequences of selecting the urgent, not important, can easily cause us to lose productivity.

Often urgent matters are not important in the long run. Here is a good rule to use when evaluating urgent versus important: Important things are usually self-directed or self-generated. These are things you can do to move your business and life forward—important things, which will have the greatest impact on you and your family: prospecting, lead follow-up calls, the appointments that you have scheduled for buyers and sellers.

"Those who make the worst use of their time are the first to complain of its brevity."
Jean De La Bruyere

The urgent matters are the phone calls from other agents, lenders, and title companies, all emotionally charged. Too often, we select the urgent over the important because someone else's emotional state influences us. When you feel yourself being swayed by someone's emotional state, take a few steps back to analyze the situation. Often people want their urgent problems to be assumed by you. Someone else causes urgent activities. By setting boundaries as to when you will be dealing with urgent activities, you will be able to accomplish much more in your allotted time.

Limiting Steps

To compact your time you must recognize the limiting steps. For every achievement or accomplishment there is a limiting step along the way. The sooner you overcome the limiting steps, the more you can accomplish. These limiting steps can create a barrier to your plans for each day. If you want to be successful, you must identify the limiting step quickly. You must focus with laser intensity on removing it.

For instance, the limiting step in prospecting might be being prepared. Often we don't have all the people we are going to call organized to begin prospecting. We then spend time in preparation when we should be on the phone. All during preparation our minds send us mental images of how hard this is going to be. By the time we get ready, we have psyched ourselves out of doing the prospecting. The preparation is the "limiting" step. The solution is to prepare today, before leaving work, for your prospecting tomorrow. That way you just walk in and do it.

If you are trying to make a flyer for a property you have listed, the limiting step could be just finding the time to drive out and take a picture of the property. Plan a time to do it, or see if you can get someone else to take the picture. Can you pay a staff person in the office a few dollars to drive out on their lunch hour to help you? Define the limiting steps in everything you do.

Time and Values

Successful people have clarity of purpose and clarity of value. They know the direction to travel and what they stand for. They have decided what is important to them. They have determined their priorities and they take action based on that order of priorities. They have also clearly defined their values, for both business and life. They are determined that their values don't conflict with work. By applying these simple steps for action and clarity you can compress your work time. You will also be able to double your effectiveness when you are at work.

> *Successful people have clarity of purpose and clarity of value. They know the direction to travel and what they stand for.*

Your Knowledge Asset

Now that we understand the value of our time and how to control it, we need to learn to increase the other asset we are selling, which is knowledge. The challenge facing all agents is acquisition of knowledge. New agents in particular must seek every opportunity to improve their knowledge and skill in real estate sales. Investing some of your time in studying and learning will yield fruit.

The Importance of Books

The average person reads less than three books after he leaves his formal schooling. That's truly a pitiful statistic for our society. No wonder the average income for a person in the United States is far less than $40,000 per year.

A study conducted on homes valued at $300,000 or greater found that eight out of ten of these homes contained one thing that homes worth less than $300,000 did not have—these homes contained a library. The question you have to ask yourself is, Did the owners just suddenly decide to get a library or did they start it years ago? Did they start that library in the corner of a small, nearly empty apartment

Enroll in the Audio University

In my early career in real estate sales I spent a minimum of two hours a day practicing scripts and dialogues that related to my listing presentations and objection handling. I am a huge believer in the audio university—listening to audiocassette tapes in your car whenever and wherever you drive. Your capacity to learn while you drive is enormous. I would spend hours daily listening to Zig Ziglar, Jim Rohn, Brian Tracy, Earl Nightingale, and many others. They helped mold and shape my thinking, my skill, and my desire.

I took to heart Jim Rohn's great thought that your formal education will make you a living but your personal education will make you a fortune. I want to say Jim is exactly right. I did not finish college or receive outstanding grades in high school. But I did invest large quantities of time starting in my mid-20s into my personal education. I can honestly say that I would not be writing this book today without those years of study. I would not have the honor to speak in front of large audiences without that personal investment. I would not get to work with some of the top agents in the country, agents who are selling 30 and 40 million dollars' worth of real estate a year.

10, 15, even 20 years ago? Did the owners buy, collect, and read good books to improve their skills, expand their thinking, define their character, and impact their life? For me that was the case. My library started in that little studio apartment. Then it moved to a one-bedroom apartment and then to a little 800-square-foot house where my wife, Joan, and I lived when we started my real estate career. When we moved into a home on a golf course, our library moved and grew with us. Then a second library was created in a vacation home where we spent three days a week.

My path to success can be yours. I believe God gave gifts for success to all of us to use. You have the seeds of greatness inside you ready to be watered and germinated and grown. The water and fertilizer are books, seminars, and audiotapes and the investment you make in yourself. With that focus your success is assured.

Are You Burning Bright or Burning Out?

Many people are heading fast toward burnout or just recovering from burnout. Burnout is a real happening for many real estate agents. We get calls from agents daily who are struggling with this dilemma. Burnout occurs when reality and our expectations don't align over time. Burnout can also trigger anger. The anger grows from the feeling

Burnout occurs when reality and our expectations don't align over time.

that life is not working out the way we had thought it would. We feel powerless to make the changes needed, or we don't know the changes that we need to implement.

There are seven key factors that can cause one to experience burnout.

Key Factor 1: We Fail to Pace Ourselves

We all have an optimum pace we need for work and life. Often we exceed that pace. We can exceed our pace for only a short period of time. When we fail to slow down and reestablish our normal pace, trouble sets in. Are you pacing yourself? What is the pace at which you are most effective at work and at home?

Key Factor 2: We Try to Do It All Ourselves

We often take on the whole world single-handedly—it's me against the world. Are you delegating all you can to others? Are your affiliates, lenders, title officers, escrow people, or home inspectors doing all they can to help you succeed? Are there services you could have your broker provide and compensate her for performing them?

Key Factor 3: We Accept Everyone Else's Problems

Too often we accept problems that are out of our control, for example, the client who "needs" a certain price for his home, the other agent's emotional or financial problems, or repair costs the seller didn't anticipate.

Key Factor 4: We Major in Minor Things

It's really easy to get worked up by the little stuff. The skill is allocating the right amount of energy and time for the size of the challenge. A good rule to follow is: If it deals with the health of you or your family or if it deals with the quality of life and relationships between you and your family, then it's big stuff. Everything else is a minor—it's small stuff.

A good rule to follow is: If it deals with the health of you or your family or if it deals with the quality of life and relationships between you and your family, then it's big stuff.

Key Factor 5: We Have Unrealistic Expectations

We live in a world filled with instant everything. We have been trained by society to want it all yesterday with no effort on our part. A recent study showed that 80 percent of the late night infomercials deal with instant weight loss or instant financial success. There are few occurrences of instant success in life. Most people have toiled for years perfecting their abilities. Measurable progress in reasonable time is the barometer by which we need to gauge our results.

Key Factor 6: We Poorly Prioritize the Important Aspects of Life

We are often so busy living we don't have time to create an abundant life. What is the most important area of your life? What area

We often are so busy living we don't have time to create an abundant life.

has more value than all others? Do your time, energy, and passion reflect the priority you need to have in that area? If you cannot answer these questions with confidence, what changes should you make to your priorities? I regard this point as being one of the biggest challenges for real estate agents. We often neglect our family for income opportunities.

Key Factor 7: We Are in Poor Physical Condition

Without a strong body, our energy and mental focus escape us. When we are in a regular exercise routine, we can relieve some of the stress that causes burnout. Prepare for the day by setting aside time in the morning or perhaps schedule a midday break. Some of us may elect an end-of-the-day stress reliever before we go home to our families.

Don't Lose Touch with Yourself

One of the major steps in avoiding burnout is to know yourself. We can often burn out if we lose touch with ourselves. There are three skills in knowing oneself. They are to know:

- your behavioral or DISC style
- your purpose
- your passion

These three areas make you an original. There is no one else like you.

Know Your Behavioral or DISC Style

DISC is a system for evaluating behavioral style. DISC stands for Dominant, Influencing, Steady, or Compliant.

Dominant: If you have a high Dominant score, you are competitive, quick to make a decision, and very results oriented.

Influencing: If you have a high Influence score, you are people oriented, warm, caring, active, in charge, and trusting of others.

Steady: If you have a high Steady score, you are nonconfrontational, stable, and want to get along with all people.

Compliant: If you have a high score in Compliant, you are systematic, accurate, numbers and data oriented, and believe facts are facts.

These styles determine your communication patterns and how you process information. The style you are affects formality, pace of speech, and body language. Knowing your style will drastically improve your effectiveness in relationships with your spouse, children, and business associates. It will also enable you to be a more effective salesperson. You will see the blind spots in your skills and abilities more clearly. Lao-tzu, the Chinese philosopher, said, "He who knows others is learned. He who knows himself is wise."

If you have never taken a DISC assessment, call us at Real Estate Champions at 541-383-8833 or e-mail us at info@realestatechampions .com and we can administer the DISC assessment.

Understand Your Purpose

My belief is that we all have a purpose to fulfill while we are here. The question is, What is yours? What is the ultimate outcome that you are trying to create in your life?

Mary Kay Ash, founder of Mary Kay Cosmetics, describes her purpose this way: to provide unlimited opportunity to women. The interesting thing is that her purpose has nothing to do with the sale of cosmetics. Purpose adds stability to life when you hit turbulent waters or when you have more opportunities than time to take advantage of them. At this point you have to be careful to select the opportunities that align with your purpose.

Know Your Passion

What causes you to get excited? What are you willing to stay up day and night for? What would you rather do than anything else in life? When you are tired, what gets you charged back up? Passion helps keep you on track. Passion also snaps you back on track when you get off track. Day-to-day pressure and wear and tear can overwhelm us when we don't have passion.

Abundance or Burnout?

Burnout is a reality we all can face again and again if we are not vigilant in watching the seven key factors. We must take action in each of these areas. Invest the time to know yourself, define your purpose, and tap into your passion. Life is meant to be spent in abundance. Are you moving toward abundance or burnout?

Your Long-Term Vision

Another hurdle in building a successful real estate sales business is creating a long-term vision for your business. Too often we are just working day-by-day and moment-by-moment. The most successful individuals are those who have a long-term vision of what their business and life will look like in 5 to 10 years.

Have a Plan on Paper

Build a vision for your business to ensure continued growth in your real estate sales. We have to have a clear objective and a defined plan to achieve our goals. Having your plan in print on paper allows you to remain consistent and true to your objectives and goals. Too often, when agents are not certain of their goals, objectives, and values, their prospects and clients will cause them to move into the gray area of their business. This gray area doesn't necessarily mean they are participating in unethical transactions, but it does mean they are adjusting their personal or core values to earn a commission check.

Know Your Core Ideology

Truly great individuals understand the difference between what should never change and what could be open for change, between what is sacred and what is not. Change is inevitable in every business. The real estate sales business is not exempt from having change forced upon it regularly. What should never change is your core ideology: that which defines your character. Your core ideology will transcend the market, technological advances, changes in brochures, the latest magic marketing gimmick. Defining who you are and what you stand for in your business will enable you to attain the success you desire.

Your core ideology consists of two main areas:

> core values
>
> core purpose

Core Values

Core values are essential to guide your business and your career. Core values are what you stand for even when no one is looking. They are what you believe in so strongly that your children are taught them. Small companies grow up to be large companies because of their adherence to their core values.

Let me share a few examples. There is a tremendous retail company in the Pacific Northwest called Nordstrom's. Nordstrom's started in 1901 as a shoe store in downtown Seattle, Washington. It started as a small business just as your real estate business is now. Nordstrom's has a core value that sets them apart:

> Service to the customer above all else.

Nordstrom's employees are world famous for their service. They will go to great lengths to ensure customer satisfaction. Many of you have probably returned items months after you bought them because they didn't measure up as garments from Nordstrom's should. Their core value of service was created decades before customer service was fashionable.

Another example is Disney. Disney's core values include creativity, dreams, and imagination. Their values produce the Fantasy Island that we get to experience. The Disney company makes fantasy seem to be reality. Walt Disney said, "If you can dream it, you can do it."

Even my company, Real Estate Champions, has core values. One of ours is the exceptional execution of the fundamentals.

Core Purpose

The second key area is core purpose. Simply stated it's why you are in real estate. Have you ever thought of why you decided to

> ## Our Core Values
>
> I believe that mastery of the fundamentals in your business leads to success. Without the mastery of fundamentals, it's only a matter of time before the house of cards falls. That's why our focus at Real Estate Champions is to help you acquire the mastery of knowledge and time management in your business. The key fundamentals in your real estate career are sales skills, time management skills, business skills, and leadership skills. I believe all other skills are secondary to these. People avoid the fundamentals because they are hard. To master the fundamentals takes work. It takes willingness to practice, learn, and put it on the line daily to achieve success. We as a company will always stand for excellence in the fundamentals. It will always be what we teach because it is a core value for our company.

enter real estate? Why did you pick this career over all the others that are available? The desire to make a lot of money is not enough of a core purpose to sustain you as a real estate agent. To be sure, the lack of money can motivate us to do certain things. But once we have solved the immediate money problem, we will be forced to reevaluate why we are doing what we do. At that time reevaluation could be harder because we have raised our standard of living. We think we can survive only on the higher income level. We then paint ourselves into a corner with fewer options. A true core purpose identifies why you are in real estate and captures the soul of your business. The core purpose does describe your income or commission volume or even the customers you are going to serve.

A true core purpose is a long statement and should not be confused with the goals you have set. Goals can be achieved but a purpose cannot. You are going to achieve your goals, cross them off, then set new ones. A purpose is a direction that you are going to work toward your whole career. The core purpose itself does not change, but it causes change. It causes change over time in goals, status, proceeds, and service that we provide. Let me share with you a few examples:

A true core purpose identifies why you are in real estate and captures the soul of your business. The core purpose does describe your income or commission volume or even the customers you are going to serve.

Wal-Mart's core purpose is to give ordinary folks the chance to buy the same things as rich people. Wal-Mart's focus is on consumers and their access to goods and services. They have built an empire on value to the consumer.

Mary Kay Ash's focus is not on men. It is not even on cosmetics. The purpose is providing unlimited opportunity to one segment of society . . . women. Mary Kay realized how hard it was to achieve success as a women in her era. She wanted to help others succeed at her level. She didn't want them to have to struggle to the top as she had.

Profit

The last major challenge is to be profitable in your business. Profit is a natural result of a well-run business. A business whose only reason for existence is money will not stand the test of time. The real focus for the business is to create and keep customers, and the profit we desire is an actual outcome of that.

Your P&L Statement

The primary tool for business is a regular profit and loss statement. Most businesses refer to this as a P&L. Having a regular P&L allows you to understand and control your expenses. The only way to properly control expenses is to know them and watch them. It's easy to expand your spending when you start to make money. Agents are famous for throwing money at anything and everything trying to acquire more business.

Define Your Core Values and Purpose

Defining your core values and core purpose will enable you to set your course in your career for years to come. They will help you remain true to your principles when money gets tight. They will ultimately attract the people who you are looking for in your business.

Expenses and Increased Service

If what you are spending money on doesn't increase the service you provide to the client, you have to question the expense. Ask yourself:

> Will it help the house sell quicker?
>
> Will it provide the seller a competitive advantage over other sellers?
>
> Will it increase the quality of the communication?

A yes answer is needed for the expenditure to be made.

Net Expenses and Profit

The other question to ask is, "Does the expense increase net profit?" This is the second reason to spend money in your business. You are making an investment for a future retirement. That return could be in dollars or in time saved by you. I once spent $3,000 on a prelisting package video that covered selling qualifications and marketing plans and how important pricing is to the sale. It allowed me to cut

Be Cautious About the Latest Gimmick

Be cautious of agents who try to convince you of the latest and greatest gadget or gimmick. They are everywhere and they always target new agents. These agents are really trying to help. For the most part, the systems or ideas they recommend were recently mentioned at some seminar. Even if they are using the techniques themselves, they usually don't know the return on profit but just thought it was a good deal at one time.

my listing presentation from about 60 to 30 minutes. When you go on 20 listing appointments a month like I did at the time, you can pay for such a video in time saved in just a month. That was a very good return on the investment I made.

Be sure to evaluate your spending well. For years, I have watched agents become successful in real estate only to find out they are making the same net profit at $250,000 as they were making at $75,000. It is easy to fall into the trap of spending as a real estate agent. Your insurance policy for not going broke is your P&L.

Act Like a Business Owner

When someone is giving you advice, always ask how it will take your business to the next level and get some cost information.

Ask them these questions.

1. How much does this service cost?
2. How much time do you or your staff have to invest in it?
3. How many transactions has this generated in the last year?
4. How many transactions did this generate in the last 30 days?
5. What is your actual investment in the project?
6. What's the commission dollar you have earned in the last year and in the last 90 days?

7. What was the biggest challenge you encountered while implementing this idea?

A business owner would ask all these questions of a salesperson before she bought the program or product.

The biggest challenge is for us to become business owners, to take control as the CEOs of our own multimillion dollar sales company. Running your real estate business as a business is a must for wealth, independence, and peace of mind. Review the material in this chapter regularly.

Mastering Your Sales Skills

Part I: Prospecting, Expired Listings, and For Sale By Owners

The X factor in your career will be the execution of your sales skills. Without exceptional sales skills you will have to continue to trade large amounts of time for your income. Good sales skills separate the most successful people and successful companies from all the others. This happens in every job, career, and profession. The most financially successful doctors, dentists, accountants, and attorneys may not be the most technically proficient, but these people have the best sales skills. In this chapter we will take an in-depth look at the sales skills you will need to develop in your first year as a real estate agent.

The IBM Model

When I was in high school and college in the late 70s and early 80s, one of the companies everyone wanted to work for was IBM. IBM prided itself on delivering the best training in the world to its salespeople. In that era if you had IBM or "Big Blue" on your resume you were employed for life. You were one of the most sought-after salespersons in the world.

In the middle 90s IBM went through a gradual transformation. They slowly demolished their wonderful sales training. Upper management was filled with accountants, engineers, and "slide rule" types. These people banded together to do away with the salespeople. They believed salespeople were beneath them. Slowly "Big Blue" was dying. Their stock took a nosedive. There were rumblings of IBM being sold, acquired, and closed. Finally, someone realized what the engineers and accountants didn't understand: Products and services are sold not bought. The IBM theory at that time was "Build it better and it will sell itself." Sadly, their thinking failed for lack of sales. They restarted the sales training and now they are back on top.

Products and services are sold not bought.

Salesmanship Is a Part of Life

I share this example because many of you are thinking that you don't want to be a salesperson. The truth is that you already are one right now. Earl Nightingale said many years ago, "We are all paid in life based on our ability to sell." Mr. Nightingale was exactly right. From the receptionist who wants a raise and has to sell it to her boss, to the spouse who wants an increase in the discretionary spending in the household budget, to the attorney who is trying to attract new clients, to your junior high schooler who is trying to convince you to increase her allowance—we are all going to be successful in life based on our ability to sell. Your effectiveness as a parent is based on your ability to sell your children on your rules and your values. For example, when you are in conflict with your children because they want to stay up later, you will usually first try to sell them on the idea of going to bed before you whip out the authority tones. Selling is a natural part of life. Developing sales skills helps you in all areas of life.

Earl Nightingale said many years ago, "We are all paid in life based on our ability to sell."

Salespeople Are the Highest Paid Professionals

At the end of the day whoever has the best sales skills wins the game. Therefore, your sales skills must be developed. I don't believe in natural-born salespeople. You can rise to the top of the

The Greatest Sale I Ever Made

The greatest sale I ever made was not a house or piece of property, nor was it a seminar or training program. The greatest sale I made was over 11 years ago convincing a woman named Joan that this ex-professional racquetball player could become something special off the court and that she should decide to spend the rest of her life with me. As long as I live, it will be the greatest sale I've made. I can tell you it wasn't the most eloquently worded presentation, but it did have passion and enthusiasm behind it. Joan was ready to buy, but some of your clients will not be. That means your words and presentation need to be a 10.

amateur level if you are gifted. But if you develop your gift, you can rise to the ranks of a professional. Salespeople are the highest paid professionals in the world. Careers in sales have produced more millionaires and multimillionaires than any other profession. You have the opportunity to earn an income that most people only dream about and few people achieve.

The Secret Ingredient: Practice

Why aren't most real estate agents in this highest paid category? Let me share with you the missing component: practice. Most agents don't practice their craft. They don't practice the words that will lead a client from sitting on the fence to a committed client relationship. If you practice using your sales skills, it will not matter what the market is doing or where interest rates are. All those outside factors will have little or no effect on your income. You can become bulletproof in your business. The name of the game is practice and most agents rarely practice. Most true professionals practice long and hard. An NFL team, for example, practices 45 to 50 times more than they play in an actual game. What would happen to our sales careers if we even did one-tenth the amount of practice these professional athletes do weekly? I have seen the results when agents adopt this challenge. Their income skyrockets. They double, triple, and even quadruple their income in less than a year. To become a sales master you have to practice your craft.

Your Key Sales Skills

The key skills we need to practice are prospecting, lead follow-up, qualifying, listing presentations, buyer interviews, objection handling, and closing techniques. These are the tools of a "top gun" agent.

Prospecting

Prospecting is essential; it's the engine that drives the train. Webster's defines prospecting as "seeking a potential buyer or customer; seeking with the vision of success." The real estate agent version for most agents is "the most unimaginable pain—worse than being boiled in oil."

We have to clearly understand that prospecting is part of the job we have selected. Many people will tell you that there is a prospect-free system to selling real estate. Sadly, they are just plain wrong. The only place where *success* comes before *work* is in the dictionary.

Your Sphere of Influence

There are many people you can prospect. Start with your sphere of influence. Your sphere of influence is all the people you know and your family knows. When you really think about it, you probably know 200 to 250 people. How about the people you went to school with, the people you know at church, the parents of your children's soccer friends, or even the people you see at your athletic club. All these are in your sphere and they all want you to succeed in your new career.

Collect information such as name, address, phone numbers (work and home), and e-mail address. Then call these people and announce that you are in business. Ask them if they know of anyone who is thinking of buying or selling real estate. Often the initial answer is no. Ask them if they would call you right away if they hear of anyone and, lastly, don't assume they will remember.

The Seven Secrets of Prospecting

For many salespeople, prospecting is the most difficult activity they do. They dread the thought of picking up the phone to make a living. However, long-term success in sales is built through solid prospecting. In order to be successful and profitable, salespeople need to apply these seven secrets of prospecting daily.

Long-term success in sales is built through solid prospecting.

1. The first call is always the most difficult. I prospected solidly for over 8 years in real estate. I never got over the difficulty of making the first call. Getting yourself to make the first call is the highest hurdle. The only solution is to just do it. After you make the first call, you realize it was not as difficult as you imagined. The person on the other end of the line was not as difficult as your imagination had made them out to be. In many cases calling begins to get fun after a few calls. The problem is most people just never break through the initial barrier.

> *After you make the first call, you realize it was not as difficult as you imagined.*

2. Establish a routine. To be successful, you should have a scheduled time for prospecting daily when that is the only activity that is being done. Treat prospecting as an appointment. Do not allow anything to interfere with your prospecting. We often allow distractions to creep into our prospecting time. The salesperson who has a set daily routine of making prospecting calls at a specific time and adheres to his schedule without distraction is guaranteed to succeed. This person will not only succeed but he will be a "top gun" agent, the best of the best.

3. Develop "Big Mo"—Momentum. At first prospecting will be very difficult. Your skills will not be developed to the level of an expert. Once you start the process, do not stop. Momentum is critical to prospecting. Once you get going, your skills will improve to generate more leads and to set more appointments. Do not break your momentum.

Another agent in the real estate office where I worked once issued me a challenge. The challenge was who could list more homes in a month. I knew I would win since I had momentum and he did not. He had not been consistently prospecting, so he had no momentum. I must say that he did have the best month he had ever had. But that was because he was consistently prospecting and had been following up on the leads he was generating. At the end of the month, my team had taken 18 listings and he had taken 6. Do not bet against "Big Mo."

4. The best time to prospect is when you have the most energy. The best time to make prospecting calls is when you have the most energy and when

Get Off to a Great Start

I always prospected early in the morning because that was when I had the most energy. It also got me off to a great start, which would carry me through the rest of the day. If I had a good, disciplined day of prospecting, then I felt I had a successful day regardless of the number of leads, number of appointments set, or anything else that happened.

you actually will call. There have been tremendous arguments over this point by agents and trainers. Set a time to prospect and call at that time. Do not worry about things you cannot control, such as someone being home or not. Focus on your skill level, avoid distractions, and prospect. These factors you can control.

5. Focus on the goal or objective. Set a specific goal of what you want to happen on each call. Know what you want that prospect to do. It is hard to achieve success in prospecting without a clearly defined objective.

The first objective is to set a qualified appointment with the prospect. If you are unable to accomplish that objective, then the next best objective is to get an agreed-upon action by the prospect within a specific time frame. For example, the prospect is going to be interviewing agents next week. You and the prospect agree to speak on Thursday about getting the appointment scheduled for next week. The last objective is to generate a lead that will buy or sell in the future. This objective depends on your definition of what a lead is for a buyer or a seller.

6. Believe in the power of scripts. Highly successful salespeople use scripts. To effectively prospect, it is crucial to know what to say before you start to prospect. Scripts provide a guide and a logical sequence of questions to follow. They allow you to focus on the response of the prospect rather than fumble around trying to find the words.

The only way to move to the highest form of communication is to know what you are going to say to the prospect. The words you say account for only 7 percent of the communication. If you know the words, you can begin to focus on your tonality and body language. Tonality accounts for 38 percent of all communication and body language accounts for 55 percent. Your body language plays a huge role in conveying energy via the phone. If you are sitting and slumped over, it's hard to generate enthusiasm and energy about anything. If you are standing up and have a little movement in your body when you prospect, you will convey passion, confidence, and conviction through your communication. On the other hand, if you are focusing and stumbling through the 7 percent of the words, you will be ineffective in prospecting. We have all heard unskilled telemarketers stumble through their scripts and dialogues. Develop, learn, and practice your scripts so you can effectively communicate and reach your prospect through your tonality and body.

7. It is a numbers game. Prospecting is truly a numbers game for two reasons. The first is the more prospecting you do, the less rejection bothers you. The best way to deal with rejection is to get as much as you can as soon as you can to reduce its effect on you. Most people you call are very nice and pleasant. They may not need your services at this time, which is fine. Rejection is rarely as bad as you imagine. The only way to find this out is to make more calls.

The second reason is you can replicate your business via numbers. Prospecting will allow you to plan your income and results. If you track your prospecting efforts, you will find you have ratios in your business. I would make 15 expired listing contacts and get a listing signed. If I wanted to list a property a day, I needed to make 15 expired contacts daily, which would then create the desired income for my family.

What is your desired income? How many prospecting contacts do you need to make to achieve it? A contact is a prospecting call that results in talking to one of the decision makers in the household. As you get more skilled, the number of contacts needed will decrease. When I first began prospecting, I needed to contact over 100 people to get a listing. Start tracking your numbers so you can play the game. To play the game well is to know and understand it.

A contact is a prospecting call that results in talking to one of the decision makers in the household.

Know the Game

Michael Jordan was the best basketball player of all time not only because of his abilities, but also because cerebrally he knew the game better than any other player. His physical skills were not at their highest levels late in his career, but his mental skills were beyond comparison. Develop your verbal and mental skills.

Develop the Habit of Prospecting

Prospecting is truly an integral part of success in any sales profession. Do not be fooled by the prospecting-free system to success. Apply the seven secrets of prospecting success. Develop the habit of daily prospecting and you will become one of the "top gun" agents in the world.

We can all learn to prospect more effectively. Make sure you find the place and the time. Don't dwell on past failures; just put them behind you. Be determined to fight for your time and fight for your focus. Create and follow a great plan of action. Be faithful to yourself and to your clients and family and finish what you start. You will find success knocking at your door in a short period of time.

Overcoming Call Reluctance

Everyone who sets out to prospect faces call reluctance. This is a natural feeling for any salesperson. I don't buy it when agents tell me they don't get call reluctance.

We are all faced with call reluctance at one time or another in our sales careers. We all know that we need to prospect and make calls daily to generate new business. Knowing and doing can be two entirely different things. The fear of calling can be a career-ender for many salespeople.

Let's take a look at what most agents do when call reluctance hits. Most agents take the worst possible action . . . they avoid initiating the calls. Are you avoiding the calls when call reluctance hits? The problem with that plan is that avoiding something out of fear only teaches you to fear it more.

Call avoidance only makes the challenge larger and harder. Your call avoidance intensifies your anxiety, which leads to greater reluctance and greater avoidance. We have all lived this pattern, leading us farther down the slippery slope of call reluctance. How do you break this pattern of destruction? Here is a five-step strategy to overcome call reluctance:

Strategy 1: Take Stock of Yourself and Your Skills

Most people who are chronic call-reluctance sufferers are their own worst enemies. They are experts in all their own faults and shortcomings. They see only their weaknesses, never their strengths. To be successful at prospecting over the phone, we have to have a clear sense of what we can provide to the prospect. Until we have a clear understanding of our own value, we will never achieve comfort in prospecting.

To be successful at prospecting over the phone, we have to have a clear sense of what we can pro-vide to the prospect.

Evaluate what you have to offer the prospect. Take inventory of your skills and abilities. Know your track record of results or your company's track record of results. Review your list of satisfied clients and the reasons why they're satisfied.

1. List the things you can do for the prospects.
2. List the qualities that make you the person they should buy from or list with.
3. List the specific benefits of your services.

Always have these lists ready by the phone so you can review them before you begin to call. You will also be able to use them during your call to convince the prospect to work with you.

Many of us are intimidated because we view making a call to a prospect or even a cold opportunity as an unwanted interruption. By using this list, you can change your mindset to see that you are giving the prospect a valuable opportunity to be served by you.

Strategy 2: Set Realistic, Achievable Daily Goals

We can easily get ahead of ourselves. By setting a daily goal that is realistic, we can create momentum. People who are challenged by call reluctance often believe that they need to make 20, 50, or even 100 calls a day to make a difference. Because they can't do that, they avoid making even one. Start with a small number you can commit to daily. We have seen agents double their businesses in a year by making 5 to 10 contacts a day. A little goes a long way.

Set manageable goals for each week, and then break them down into a goal for each day.

Prospecting is like Brill Cream: A little dab'll do ya. It just has to be used every day.

Set manageable goals for each week, and then break them down into a goal for each day. If you are struggling to hit the daily goal, break it down to each part of the day, or even each hour, if necessary.

Strategy 3: Control Negative Self-Talk

We all have an internal voice. Sometimes that voice is our biggest fan and cheerleader. Other times it feels like that little voice is chaining us to a cement block and pushing us into a deep river. That internal voice can encourage us; it can criticize and chastise us as well.

For those of you who are regularly challenged by call reluctance, this negative self-talk can be particularly aggressive. It can become almost paralyzing when you are preparing for a sales call. When you are going to pick up the phone, the negative self-talk turns up the volume and intensity.

Reward Yourself

Make it into a game. How many calls can I make before lunch or before my next appointment at 10:00? Make the target achievable. You want to have a feeling of accomplishment. When you achieve the goal, reward yourself. We call it celebrating the victory. Part of being effective in calling is learning to reward yourself along the way. The mouse wouldn't work as hard to get to the end of the maze if the cheese weren't there. The reality is that we are no different. You have to create small rewards along the way.

"She is going to reject you."

"Why would he use you instead of these other agents."

"Maybe there is another way to do this."

"I should really be handling a problem transaction."

"I need to do more research before I make this call."

Meet the challenge of the negative self-talk head on. If you do, the voice will get quieter, and after a few dials it will go away completely.

If you are really struggling, write down what the negative self-talk is saying. By having the words down on paper, you can refute what is being said in your mind. The only way to repel the voice is to create the responses that defuse the arguments. It's the difference between your thoughts controlling you and you controlling your thoughts. You must take charge of this challenge.

Strategy 4: Visualize the Perfect Call

We often begin each call by envisioning rejection. We begin each call with the thought, "I hope they're not home." Do you visualize them hanging up in disgust, or is there a voice telling you they will be happy to hear from you? We often have a horrible movie playing in our head. Those negative images make the calls more difficult to execute.

We can create the outcome before we ever pick up the phone. Those negative visions create self-fulfilling prophecies and we get caught going through the motions without achieving the results we desire. There are two key reasons we end up short of the outcome we planned for:

1. **The negative visions generate stress and the mental stress blocks performance.** We are preoccupied with the stress. We are waiting for the other shoe to drop so we can be right.
2. **The negative visions are a rehearsal.** The more you run the negative through mentally, the greater the probability of reproducing it in reality. You will create the outcome you visualize.

We must visualize ourselves talking on the phone with confidence. We must have a "bring it on" attitude. We must visualize ourselves handling the objections efficiently and effectively, and we must visualize ourselves setting an appointment.

Strategy 5: Use the "Ten-Minute Strategy"

It's really easy when you are in call reluctance to envision hours of calling and toiling on the phone. You believe that you are going to have to bear hours of rejection to generate one measly lead. Then you figure you might as well give yourself the day off and you can make it up tomorrow.

Resolve before you give up for the day to make calls for 10 minutes. Any of us can make calls for just 10 minutes! When you have completed 10 minutes or a certain number of contacts, like two or three, you can quit guilt-free. You have "bought" your freedom for the day. You have taken a big step to breaking through call reluctance. Do the 10-minute drill and know you are progressing out of call reluctance.

Call Reluctance Is Real

You will discover that the hardest part is behind you. You can tap into the momentum you have just created. I guarantee that the next dial will be easier and not feel intimidating. You have started to control the negative self-talk. You can choose to continue on. This is the best commitment you could make and keep for yourself.

Call reluctance is real for every salesperson. There is no one who doesn't suffer from some form of call reluctance. If some claim they

Referrals Can Come from Unexpected Places

I had a coaching client recently who was one of the best agents in his market. He had been selling real estate for more than 10 years and never had gotten a referral from his mother. I asked him if he ever prospected her and asked her to send him a referral. He said, "No, I didn't think I would have to remind my mother that I am in real estate sales." My response was for him to call her and ask for referrals. Two weeks later he called me and said she had given him two referrals in the last two weeks. It wasn't merely a coincidence—it was because he asked. "Ask and you will receive" is true. Prospecting is the process of asking.

don't ever have it, just realize they must have deeper psychological problems to deal with. Apply the five steps today, and work to overcome call reluctance.

Expired Listings

Expired listings are another excellent source of prospecting opportunities. These are listings that were with another agent who failed to sell the home. For most of these people it is still urgent to sell. Most of them have not selected another agent to represent them.

Expireds are a great option. They have already raised their hand and announced to the world that they want to sell.

A vast majority of agents never call these people to apply for the job of selling their home. In my market, there were more than 7,000 active licensed agents. I would say less than 100 agents worked the expired market with regularity rather than try to find people who wanted to buy and sell in a larger untested group.

Expireds are a great option. They have already raised their hand and announced to the world that they want to sell. Your only job is to call them and ask for an appointment. It is very difficult to convince anyone today to do business with you over the phone. Your objective is to set up an appointment with all the decision makers present to make a presentation in person.

Call Consistently

Your objective is to call consistently until they list or die! Too often we stop short of the mark. You need to call until you are certain they will never list their home. Often the expired will give you the "reflex

Phone call consistency is essential for success in the expireds.

no" because of the volume of calls they are receiving from others. The "reflex no" is a no that is given without thought. Let me give you an example: You go into a department store and the clerk asks if she can help you. Your immediate response is, "No, I'm just looking." That is a "reflex no." Even though you go to the store to buy something, you have learned to give that response to disengage the salesperson. The expired will often give you a "reflex no" and hope you will never call back. They will often tell you they will never put their home on the market again and next week you see it has been listed.

Phone call consistency is essential for success in the expireds. Calling the new expireds every other day for a week or every day for a week is essential. Don't assume they will remember you, because they won't. I have called people back even after helping them for 10 minutes with their home and they don't know me from all the other calls they have received. One element of skillful prospecting is to be there at the right time. The only way to ensure that is to call often and ask for the appointment.

How to Make Six Figures Prospecting Expired Listings

Prospecting expired listings can be the core of anyone's business in the real estate field. You can create a system that will give you repeatable results for your effort. Let's look at these three characteristics of prospecting expired listings.

1. **They are easy to find.** The expired listings come up every day. You will always have a handful that you can work on. Expired listings provide a steady stream of new leads of people to contact for listing appointments. There are usually a few very heavy days in each month. Set your schedule to take advantage of these days. The end of the month is usually one of the heaviest times for expired listings; up to 25 percent of the expired listings for the month may come up on a heavy day.

2. **They want to sell.** The expired listings were on the market at one time, unlike many other types of clients. They had a plan laid out to sell and move. Their plan did not work out and in most cases they wish it had. There will be some expireds that were listed by people who are now tired of the process, but the majority of them still want to sell.

3. **The bulk of them are looking for an agent.** If the expireds still have the desire to sell, as most do, they may be ready to consider changing agents. They are looking for someone who can solve their problem. Most do not know why their home did not sell, but they are frustrated with their previous agent and sometimes all agents. They will rarely return to their previous agent.

The CAP System

The successful way to work expired listings is the CAP system.

consistency

attitude

persistence

1. The first part is consistency. You must consistently work the expired listings. To achieve a large return on the time you have invested, you must work diligently for a minimum of 4 weeks straight. Expired listings cannot be started and stopped without losing momentum. There is a rhythm and a flow to expireds. They must be one of the daily disciplines that you work on. If you prospect them for 2 weeks and take a week off, *you are back to zero.* I did not prospect weekends, but I did call diligently Monday through Thursday.

Create a Pipeline of Expireds

Your leads must build, and your follow-up must grow. When you get down the road in 30-plus days, you will begin to receive calls for listing appointments from your work earlier in the month plus your appointments from new expireds. You must work to create a pipeline of expired listing clients.

2. The second part is attitude. Your attitude plays a crucial role in your success with expired listings. You need to convey to the sellers an attitude of compassion and problem solving. They are not just looking for someone to pound a sign in the ground. They are looking for someone to get their home sold. They are looking for someone to solve their problem. They feel that everyone else is the problem, when it may be them, the condition of their home, or their price. They can get even more resentful because of the high volume of agents who call them.

The price is the problem 90 percent of the time when it comes to expired listings. Too many agents who work with expireds hit their prospective clients with a ball pein hammer between the eyes about the price. That will work with some and fail miserably with others. You must be able to adjust your delivery.

You need to read the prospective clients, but most importantly you need to exude an attitude of caring and compassion for their situation while conveying confidence in your ability to get the job done. Sometimes the only way to get the price down is to convince them you care and it pains you that they have to sell for less, but there is no other way. It is like the doctor who tells his patient she has cancer. He does not like it, but he has to do it so he can start trying to cure her.

3. The last, and most critical, is persistence. Your persistence, or ability to stick to it, can have the most positive results of all. Many of the expired listings do not set appointments right away with agents. Sellers will wait a week or two or a month. The amount of calls they receive about their home drops dramatically as the weeks tick by. Do not be one of the agents who lose interest, unless the sellers have low motivation or are unreasonable. Be one of the ones left standing at the end of a week or two.

Call them a few times a week. All you are doing is trying to set an appointment. You are not doing a listing appointment over the phone. Just close for an appointment. That is what the call is for. You just want to be one of the three or four agents they interview. If you keep that as your goal, you will get plenty of salable listings.

Focus on the CAP system daily. Work both today's expired listings and the past ones daily. Effectively follow up with your hot leads daily. Remember consistency, attitude, and persistence are the keys to success in making six figures in prospecting expired listings.

For Sale by Owner (FSBO)

FSBOs are wonderful sources of revenue. They, like the expireds, have announced to the world they want to sell. They are most likely going to hire an agent to sell their home . . . they just don't know it yet! The first week an FSBO comes on the market, with their signs up and their ads in the newspaper, they think selling their home is easy and they don't need you. They can even be hostile to agents at that time. Don't take it personally. Your job is to wait them out. In most markets, less then 20 percent of the FSBOs sell. That leaves 80 percent for agents to work.

To work FSBOs well you have to track them. You can track them through their ads. Use their telephone number and the area they live in as the tracking reference. They will change their ad, but rarely change their phone number. By collecting the ads they are running weekly you can track how long they have been trying on their own. Usually an FSBO will be getting tired of trying to sell around the fourth to sixth week on the market. You must stay consistent in your weekly follow-up until then.

Drop By to See the House

One technique for creating a connection with FSBOs is to drop by to see the house. Here is an effective script to use:

> Mr. _____, I am trying to stay on top of everything that is on the market. Would you be offended if I stopped by to take a quick look at your home?

Their natural response to your request for an appointment to list the home would be no, but because of the way this question is worded, the no actually turns into a yes and you have an appointment to see the home. You then give them an option of times to set an appointment with you. When you reach the house, the goal is not to list it. The goal is to find out how soon they want to move, where they are moving to, and if they don't sell in the next 30 days what is their plan. Also, find out if they are going to interview agents at that time, and if so, ask them if you could be one of the agents they interview. Remember, your first objective in every selling situation is to gain the interview.

How to Add More Than Six Figures to Your Income Prospecting FSBOs

FSBOs can be uncomfortable for real estate agents to work with. They can often be extremely rude and inconsiderate. They also can be a great source of income if handled in the appropriate manner. The reality is, you do not have to look for them . . . they are out there. They are advertising in the newspaper saying, "Come list me."

> *Remember, your first objective in every selling situation is to gain the interview.*

The first task we have is to understand the FSBO. They have a specific reason for trying to sell on their own. We as agents need to find out that reason. In nine out of 10 instances the primary reason is to save on the commission. The other reasons are low motivation, the belief that real estate agents as a group are incompetent, or their ego (because their neighbor or friend got lucky it must be easy). Some of these reasons are hard to get around. In many cases, low motivation and ego are cause enough to move on to another potential client.

Be Picky

In working FSBOs I subscribe to the three P's theory: picky, patience, and persistence. You must work these three P's in some combination to be successful in FSBOs. The first, and I believe the most important P, is being picky. You must be highly selective in working FSBOs. One of the first mistakes I made early in my career was trying to work too many FSBOs at a time. They must be screened very carefully and completely.

The more you exclude the difficult or unreasonable FSBOs, the more time you will have to devote to the enjoyable people you can work with. You are not going to list them all. Focus on the really motivated and good people whom you will enjoy working with. This will allow you to do more business with less effort. Life is too short to work with people whose expectations for you will always be unattainable.

How Strong Is Their Motivation?

The FSBOs need to be screened for motivation. You are looking for the ones who *have* to sell, not those who just *want* to sell. They have to move for a valid reason, not just because they feel like it. The feeling may not be strong enough for them to invest 6 to 7 percent of their equity in your fees. This is clearly their mindset. This mindset is false, but often they feel that it is very valid. They feel they are losing money. The truth is they were never going to get the money in the first place. They need to be motivated to sell because they are transferring, having a new child, divorcing, needing a one-level house due to health, or some other clearly defined reason. They have no option but to sell and sell *right now*.

Will They Require High Maintenance?

Once you have a motivated seller, you need to determine his maintenance level. You must decide if the seller is high maintenance or low maintenance. High maintenance FSBOs will cause you to lose money. You need to be able to spot them and exclude them from being one of your clients. They will call you at all hours of the day and night and bother you incessantly. They often will try to tell you how to do your job. This pestering can be an ongoing drain of time and energy for both you and your staff. It is only one deal—what are you willing to do for one deal? FSBOs often know just enough to be dangerous to themselves and others. They, however, do not realize this fact until it is too late. You must evaluate the owner before you take the listing. Do you want to be associated with this person for at least 60 days and more like 120 to 180 days until the deal is closed and you are paid?

How Great Is Their Integrity?

The next evaluation I make is based on integrity. Do the sellers have the integrity to tell the truth regarding the condition of their home? Are they going to be honest with you or are you the enemy just looking for a commission? You do not need to do business with people who have this attitude. Rarely will you create a win/win situation with people who have this philosophy of life.

Be Patient

Another key to success in working with FSBOs is patience. You need to patiently wait them out. They will all run their course. They all have a certain length of time they will endure in the process of selling on their own. The key is to find out that length of time and be there at the appointed hour.

Most of the FSBOs will not think about listing until they have tried selling for 3 to 6 weeks. They want to give it a good try before giving up. The higher the motivation, the shorter the time they will try the FSBO route. Therefore, your follow-up will need to be more aggressive with the motivated ones.

Your patience factor needs to be great because you know you can help them. You have to let them fall and then help them get back up. It is almost like watching your children go through the process of taking their first steps or riding a bike for the first time. Early on I wanted to teach FSBOs and help them before they were ready. It was painful to watch them create all these problems for themselves. But they did not want my insight or help at that time. If you move in too early and too hard, you are out the door. You need to patiently wait till they go through the whole cycle. When they finally realize they cannot do it themselves, then you can step in and help.

Your goal is not to convince them to list with you, but just to interview you.

At that moment you must step in aggressively and decisively. You cannot hesitate once they get to this point.

Be Persistent

The last principle is persistence. You must stick in there with calls, letters, updates, and other communications. The goal of persistence is to be one of the three or four agents they interview for the job. Your goal is not to convince them to list with you, but just to interview you. Just like expireds, they get fewer calls from agents as the weeks go by. If you maintain a steady professional level of contact for three or four weeks, you will usually get an interview. Continue to contact them and continue to follow up on their progress. Let them know you are there to provide a quality service if they have the need for it.

The Importance of Qualifying FSBOs

If you have been picky and have qualified them well, you can be less patient and less persistent. This means that if they are more motivated, you will spend less time and money on follow-up mail pieces and phone calls to them. Their window for marketing the home as a FSBO is small. They will try for a few weeks and then turn it over to you.

I cannot impress upon you enough how critical qualifying can be. The biggest loss is the client you list who turns out to be a nightmare. She can disrupt or ruin the whole day for you. You also lose all the time and money you have invested when they do not sell or when you release them because they are not worth it. Make that selection very wisely. You are going to spend time, effort, and energy on every listing you take. Make sure you get compensation for your efforts.

FSBOs can be a wonderful source of income for many of you. You must look at them as a valid set of clients who truly need help; they just do not know it yet. By applying the three P's, you will be able to add a fourth P—high *profit*! That fourth P is the most important P in any business.

Advantages of FSBOs and Expireds

For Sale By Owners and Expireds Are Excellent Sources of Revenue

1. Most agents don't work them, so there is little competition.

2. They have announced that they want to sell.

3. They will force you to acquire the skill of sales. Many agents overlook this point. People who are successful in these disciplines

are the best salespeople in real estate. They have the ability to make convincing and compelling presentations. They also have the skill to overcome the objections of the seller. If you truly want to be the best in the real estate field, these two areas will forge your skills like no other.

4. Once you master these two groups, you will be marketproof. Many agents' income is tied to the increase of the market. If the market goes up, they make more money. If the market softens, they make less. Being successful in the expireds and FSBOs creates success in all market situations.

When the market is up and inventory for listings is tight, there will be few expired listings because all the listed homes are selling. This will cause more people to try to sell their home on their own, so there will be an abundance of FSBOs. When the market is falling and homes are difficult to sell, there will few FSBOs. Most people will feel that if the agents can't sell them why should they try on their own. In that market there will be a lot of expireds. There will be many homes that failed to sell. If you master FSBOs and expireds you can earn a fantastic living in any market.

Mastering Your Sales Skills

Part II: Leads and Effective Listing Presentations

Lead Generation

We are in the lead generation business. If you want to take control of your life and your business at a greater level, you must set up a lead generation system. This system should be designed to generate large quantities of leads. By always having great quantities of leads, you can be highly selective in the people you work with. You will only be able to help a handful of people with regularity.

These few people should be the best and most motivated clients and the ones who are sold on you and your service.

What Is a Lead?

One of the critical questions to ask yourself is, What is a lead? What is your definition of a *lead?* Each person's definition will tell a great deal about where he is in the business. When I first started, my definition of a lead was someone who wanted to buy or sell. It was a very simple definition. It was also a very broad definition and excluded very few people. My definition today would be someone who wants to buy or sell in the next 14 days. My definition has changed dramatically over the years. How did I get from one very broad definition to one that was quite narrow? Let's take a look at the process.

> *When I first started, my definition of a lead was someone who wanted to buy or sell. It was a very simple definition. It was also a very broad definition and excluded very few people.*

You Can Have Too Many Leads

Like most new agents, I had very little knowledge of the business. I was chasing after any and every deal I could find. Because my definition or philosophy about a lead was so broad, everybody on the face of the earth was qualified as a potential client. Because everyone qualified as a potential client, I had too many to work with. Most of my potential "clients" honestly would never buy or sell a home, let alone one through me.

I spent a tremendous amount of time trying to persuade people to buy or sell who really never were going to buy or sell. I decided to tighten my definition to anyone who would buy or sell within a year, then to anyone who would buy or sell within six months, then within 60 days, 30 days, and finally 14 days. If I had tightened my definition from the beginning, I would have saved myself a lot of mistakes, anguish, and lost income.

Cultivate Now Business

Do not hesitate to clearly define a *lead* in terms of *now* business. Spend the additional time working to find more leads through prospecting. Having a few good leads is better than having a bunch of marginal ones. Quality versus quantity is the name of the game. If your desire is to sell a home a week, you need only two to three *now* leads weekly to accomplish your goal. Think in terms of qualified people who want to do something *now!*

All the time I spent working with people who were too far out cost me a lot of money. We have all spoken with many people or even shown them property when they did not have the motivation to buy or sell *now!* Do not continue that process—change today!

Having a few good leads is better than having a bunch of marginal ones. Quality versus quantity is the name of the game.

Now Clients Versus Project Clients

You must clearly state your definition of a lead. Here is a little hint for you: It should be someone who wants to buy or sell in 60 days or less. Any further out and you are not creating closings for the near future. You are investing your time, your most precious commodity, in someone who may not buy or sell. Do not

Hang On to the Good Leads

There are people who want to buy and sell today; our job is to find them and help them do it. My goal was to list or sell a home every day. My job every morning when I got up was to find that person every working day. It is no more complicated than that. I would find people who were 2 weeks away, 10 days away. If I filled my pipeline with these people, I always had great leads to work with. I did not have lots of leads, but the ones I had were highly motivated and I was confident I would get a listing or sale in the next week or two by combining sales skills and effective follow-up. You might call it relentless follow-up. Do not let go of a good lead. Have you ever tried to get a bone away from a big dog? Develop that attitude with good leads.

waste your time for anyone or anything. We are all given only so much time in life. You and I have only so many days, so do not waste them with people whom we cannot help.

If you have too many potential clients rather than *now* clients, you will have a high level of frustration and no control of your business, not to mention the financial losses you will face. Keep your number of long-term or "project clients" down so you can invest your time finding people who need help now. I define *project clients* as those who are:

1. Looking for the "perfect house." I guarantee they will never find it.

2. Looking for a "tremendous deal." The deal rarely is good enough for them to move today. If the deal is so tremendous, some other smart agent has bought it already.

3. Waiting for the right house so they can put their home on the market. If they do not become motivated to sell after you show them a few houses that meet their criteria, you need to reevaluate whether they will sell in the near future.

4. Still not motivated after you call them back a few times.

We have all spent large amounts of money on mailings to people who are not moving. We have also spent large amounts of time following up on poor leads. Stop working with people who are not committed to doing something *now*. The old belief that "great salespeople should be able to sell ice to an Eskimo" is false. Great salespeople have clear definitions of what constitutes a lead. They clearly follow their narrow definitions. They prospect enough to keep a constant supply of leads flowing, so they can qualify and define them carefully.

Separate the Wheat from the Chaff

As it says in the Bible, Jesus separated the wheat from the chaff, gathering his wheat into the barn and burning up the chaff. We must separate the good kernels of *now* clients from the chaff of unmotivated sellers and buyers. The kernels of wheat have value, the chaff has no value. The wheat will feed your body and mind. The chaff will provide zero nourishment.

When you do not separate effectively, you get too bogged down with future business that never happens, or worse, you miss the *now* clients or do not have the time to find them because you are hoping this future business will work out. You often feel like you have so much invested in future business that you cannot just cut your losses even though in your heart you know it is right. Always remember the least painful loss you will take is the one taken today.

Stick to Your Definition of a Lead

Take the time today to reflect and clearly define what a lead is to you. Review your definition every quarter to see if it has changed. Stick to your guns. Do not compromise because most of the time you will be burned. There is nothing more painful than to compromise and then not get paid for your effort. Once in a while you will find that person you excluded will buy or sell with someone else. More often than not, you just saved yourself time and frustration.

> *Great salespeople do not worry about the transaction or the closing they never had. They focus on the key four-letter word in sales,* next.

Above all do not be concerned if you made a mistake by overqualifying or overdefining, which causes someone to use another agent. Great salespeople do not worry about the transaction or the closing they never had. They focus on the key four-letter word in sales, *next*.

The 80/20 Rule

There is another way I use to categorize people and leads. It's a rule I used early on in my real estate sales career. It will help ensure that you select the correct people to work with. This is the Pareto principle or the 80/20 rule.

We have all been exposed to the 80/20 rule—80 percent of our results come from 20 percent of our labor, or 80 percent of our income will come from 20 percent of our prospects. When this rule is learned and applied, it is a powerful tool for success.

The 20/50/30 Rule

Another rule is more powerful but less known than the 80/20 rule. It is the 20/50/30 rule. Let's take an in-depth look at this rule.

People Who Already Trust You

In the 20/50/30 rule, the 20 percent are made up of the people who will do business with you easily. This 20 percent represent people with whom you have already built trust and rapport. They have faith that what you say is true. They believe that you are skilled at what you do, and they would be pleased to work with you. They often treat professionals in other fields with respect. This type of client and prospect is like gold. This 20 percent is a pleasure to do business with. They can come from any source, such as open houses or prospecting. They could also be past clients or referrals.

People Who Are on the Fence

The next group is the 50 percent who are on the fence. This group, upon receiving a solid presentation and systematic approach, move towards your side of the fence. But it takes sufficient data and reasoning to get them to commit to buying or selling a home. This group, after careful evaluation of the data, will make a decision based on how it will benefit them. Having a benefit-based listing presentation is crucial to landing this type of prospect. You just need to apply solid sales skills and these prospects will become like the "golden" 20 percent.

The Highly Demanding People

The final group, which is the group 30 percent of people fall into, is the most challenging and dangerous group. This group demands tremendous amounts of energy and time to convince them to join your side of the fence. This 30 percent is highly demanding and often has limited respect for the services provided by others. Even with a solid service presentation, they often demand more from a salesperson than the other two groups do.

Once I had determined an individual was in this 30 percent, I would disregard the lead because the conversion rate in this group is very low. A large amount of time can be invested on people in this 30 percent, but it will equate to low payoff and high frustration. I doubt if this group can be satisfied even if everything goes perfectly. My advice is run away from prospects and clients in this group, fast!!

Concentrate on the 20 Percent and the 50 Percent

We, as salespeople, cannot help everyone. Why not simply focus first on the easy 20 percent, the 20 percent that are truly in your corner rooting for you? In addition, move to the 50 percent, which will require a little selling of yourself and the benefits of working with you. These two categories will provide more income, less frustration, and more enjoyable experiences.

Next time you speak with a prospect or client ask yourself three questions. The first question is, Which category is she in? Next ask how can I move her into the 20 percent if she is not already in it? And finally, how much effort and energy will I invest in moving her to the 20 percent? Once you have asked these questions, determine what the odds are that she will convert. Ask yourself, is the effort worth the reward? By asking these questions you will be applying the 20/50/30 rule effectively.

Categories of Leads

AA Lead = the prospect will buy or sell in 30 days or less

A Lead = the prospect will buy or sell in 60 days or less

B Lead = the prospect will buy or sell in 120 days or less

C Lead = the prospect will buy or sell in 120 days to one year

Classify Your Follow-Up

Now that you have defined all your leads, your next step is to build a follow-up system. The follow-up system needs to be focused around contact by phone, mail pieces, and e-mail correspondence. The higher the motivation of the lead, the more frequent and personal your contact with them. Personal contact is to be completed either by phone or in person.

AA Leads—Will Buy or Sell in 30 Days or Less

Call them at least three times a week.

Send at least one e-mail or mail piece weekly.

Repeat the process until they purchase or list their home or until they drop to another lead category. You can't follow up enough on these people. Even if you were to call a buyer lead just to say, "I looked twice today on the multiple listing service and nothing came up that matched your criteria for homes. If I can do anything for you please give me a call," your client would appreciate your persistence and feel he has the best agent on the job. Make sure you call, call, and call again on these AA Leads.

A Leads—Will Buy or Sell in 60 Days or Less

Call at least once a week, just to check in and ask for an appointment.

Send a piece of mail weekly.

These are the people you are percolating so they can move to the higher category. Make sure you don't neglect them, as they have a high probability of becoming an AA lead.

B Leads—Will Buy or Sell in 120 Days or Less

Call them every 3 to 4 weeks.

Send a piece of mail to them once a month.

In many cases, these B Leads need to be realistic about the value of their property and pricing or what they can afford to purchase. The people who are forever in this category must be avoided; for example, those who are trying to find the perfect house will rarely find it. There are people who look at homes regularly who would move if they could sell their current residence for $30,000 over market and could buy at $25,000 below market. Often these people will even feel they are doing you a favor by having you look for properties for them. My advice is simply this: Don't waste your time. These people rarely buy or sell. The conditions will never be "just right."

C Leads — Will Buy or Sell in 120 Days to One Year

Call them every 2 months to see if their plans are still
    on track.

Put them in any regular mailing you do, for example,
    your quarterly newsletter.

Because someone "feels like moving" is not a good enough reason for you to keep the lead long term.

For C Leads to be any good, they need to be planning to buy or sell at a specific time in the future. We can fill our databases up with pseudo-leads that are "thinking" of selling next year. To be a qualified C lead, there should be a specific reason. For example, they are retiring and want to downsize, or their last child is graduating from high school. There should be some event coming up in their life that will trigger the move. Because someone "feels like moving" is not a good enough reason for you to keep the lead long term. People who say, "We are thinking about making a move next June," and there is no reason given, don't warrant very much attention!

Create an Effective Lead Follow-Up System

Lead follow-up costs you time, time that could be spent prospecting, creating strategic alliances, or practicing your skills. Your ability to categorize your leads and follow up will help you control the leads you have right now. Creating an effective lead follow-up system can be the backbone to a consistent real estate sales business. The more effectively you handle the leads you generate, the more production you will achieve.

Too many agents spend too much time trying to find the leads they generated. They know the leads are on their desk somewhere. You need to be able to put your hands on your leads immediately when needed.

Software for Tracking Leads

One of the best ways to track leads is by contact management software programs. These programs are designed to help you keep information that will enable you to sell more efficiently and effectively. There are many on the market, some of the best are ACT!, Top Producer, and Online Agent. Select a system you are comfortable with and be certain it will grow with you and your business.

Your broker may already have a system for the whole office, as many companies are now providing this service to agents. The most important element is knowing how to use it fully. Get the training you need to master this technology that will allow you to handle the leads you generate easily and quickly.

A Low-Tech Tracking System

If you are unable to afford a computer and software, you can track leads manually with 3 × 5 note cards in a shoebox. I tracked my leads this way when I started in real estate sales many years ago. Sometimes we can get too fancy and technical for our own good. We become excited about all the new technology and gadgetry and forget "old-fashioned" sales skills. The key is to meld the technology with quality sales skills. By doing this you will achieve spectacular results.

If you have to do lead follow-up manually, get a set of cards for the 12 months. Then get another set of cards for the days of the week (Monday through Friday) or dates (the first through the thirty-first). Use the two systems together. Use the month cards for the month you have to call the prospect back. When that month arrives, use the dated cards. Move your leads to the date that you want to call them. Then write notes on your conversations and information about the client or prospect on the 3×5 card.

Qualifying

Understanding what are leads and what are not leads will keep you on track for your daily prospecting. Qualifying will also ensure you are always working with people who can buy or sell today.

The process of qualifying is a lost art in the sales profession, and this is especially true in real estate. We often work with people with low motivation hoping we can convince them to do something. In the end we spend large amounts of time working with people who don't buy or sell. Then we de-motivate ourselves because the outcome is not what we desired. We beat ourselves up because of lack of success and lack of income. We put ourselves in such a negative state that when a good buyer or seller comes along we are not prepared to seize the moment and help him. This causes us to miss another opportunity to grow our business and provide for our families. It is a vicious cycle, one that must be broken.

The Problem with Too Many Leads

Qualifying effectively determines whether the leads are good or bad. Most people don't realize that leads can be bad. Ultimately, having too many leads can be bad for your business. It can cause you to get bogged down in lead follow-up and never get back to generating of new leads through prospecting.

Too many leads can cause you to become complacent—comfortable with the probability of future income. For example, we have 25 leads that are uncategorized and unqualified. Most agents would feel very good. Some would stop prospecting for leads and they would just work those 25. The mistake is that we have not qualified. We really don't know if these leads have any value.

Determine Who Is Going to Act Now

The best agents are highly skilled at qualifying. They can quickly separate the wheat from the chaff when it comes to prospects. Being able to determine who is going to act now versus act soon versus never act at all is critical. Most new agents are just trying to do a deal rather than make sure it's the right deal to do.

Most agents treat all the leads the same with the result that the most motivated ones are missed. We don't want to annoy anyone, so the most motivated people slip through our follow-up system and buy or sell with someone else. Now we are down to 22 leads. These 22 leads are still not motivated enough to do anything. But because we lost the others we don't want to lose these so we hold on to them for dear life. The problem still remains because they are never going to do anything. We spend too much time working with unmotivated people. We have stopped prospecting, so there are no new leads. We have now come to a dangerous point in our business. For these reasons, you must make sure you qualify every prospect and client to ensure you gain a return from your time invested and never stop prospecting.

To Qualify a Seller

To qualify the seller effectively you need a series of questions to ensure their motivation is right and to prepare you for the listing presentation. Here are the key questions we recommend:

1. How soon do you want to be in your new home? This question focuses on time frame and motivation. It also gives you an opportunity to create a sense of urgency. If they say "in 60 days" and the average market time in your area is 70, you have an opportunity to talk urgency of listing tonight and getting going because they are behind. They need 30 days to close the deal once they are under contract and 70 days on average to sell it. We are 40 days behind where we need to be. We don't have a minute to waste!

2. How much do you want to list your home for? This question reveals the motivation of the client. The higher the price over what is fair market value, the lower the motivation. Sometimes clients will not tell you. They feel they don't want to tip their hand. If that is the case, then ask: What are you planning to invest in your next home?

3. What are you hoping to net after the sale of this home? This will give you what you need. We are trying to understand their feelings of value for their property. It is rare when someone does not have an idea of what they want to sell for.

4. So I can prepare a new sheet, how much do you owe on the property? I want to be able to use the net profit to help them. I also now know how much they want to list their home for even if they don't tell me. It's a great way to learn their price.

5. Have you thought about selling yourself? This will tell you if you are going to face the commission objection. Also, they may just want a price opinion from you and never want to list. We don't need to waste our time with this information-service type of client.

6. Are you interviewing other agents? It's important to know the agents and the firms you are competing against. Knowing your competition you have a competitive advantage. You can accentuate the services your company provides that the other companies don't. If you are up against a very successful agent, you can sell personal service and attention. You can assure your clients that you can spend a greater amount of time accomplishing the sale of their home.

7. What are the most important criteria for selecting an agent? You want to know what they feel is important. People have different reasons for hiring agents and you need to know theirs. Often they will tell you price of the home or commission. You want to make sure you go beyond those two. Get at least two criteria to address on the presentation.

Qualifying the seller before the appointment is a non-negotiable component in successful selling. Don't waste your time going to an appointment with the wrong type of seller. These questions should be asked over the phone 24 hours before the appointment to list their property. Practice the qualifying scripts and process daily. Don't be one of the many agents who struggle with selecting the right client in the first place.

To Qualify a Buyer

We invest large amounts of time with buyers. There is nothing more frustrating than spending a lot of time with buyers and never getting paid for our efforts. The key component to successfully working with buyers is the qualifying process. Qualifying is the lost art of the sales

Separate the Motivated Buyers and Sellers

The key in sales is the ability to separate the unmotivated buyers and sellers from the motivated ones who want to do something now. Top-producing agents know how to do this quickly and efficiently. They have a specific step-by-step series of questions that remove the unmotivated people from their lives.

Sometimes we get so excited that we have a lead that we fail to determine its value. That is why the process of qualifying is focused on determining the value of leads.

process. Sometimes we get so excited when we have a lead that we fail to determine its value. That is why the process of qualifying is focused on determining the value of leads. Here are some questions to use in qualifying a buyer.

1. How long have you been looking for a home? The object is to find out their time frame and level of passion to move. The longer the time the buyer has been looking, the lower the motivation. We have to wonder why a buyer has not been able to find a home in 6 months. Are they looking for something that doesn't exist? Are their expectations too high for the marketplace? Do they just enjoy the process of kicking foundations? When someone says to me that she has been looking for more than 90 days, I want to know what she is looking for and the reasons why she hasn't found it yet.

2. Do you need to sell your current home before you can buy? The follow-up question is, "Are you currently on the market?" Most people need to sell their home before they can buy, but a great percentage of them want to find a house before they put theirs on the market. This approach seems to be backward. Most sellers truly can't buy anything because they have to sell first. They often want us to invest a large percentage of our time finding them the perfect home prior to listing theirs.

3. Are you working with another agent? Too often we rush out to show one of our listings only to find out the clients are working with another agent. We just spent 30 minutes of our time and never got compensated.

In my career I have received some unbelievable responses from prospects regarding why they hadn't contacted their own agent about showing them property. Responses ranged from "My agent is out of town" to "I did not want to bother him." They wanted to bother me and then get *their* agent to write the sales agreement if they decided to purchase it. Our policy was, if buyers are working with another agent, he can show them the home. That is what their agent is getting paid to do.

Buyers Become Sellers

One of our rules when I was an agent was that buyers had to list their property at the time for us to work with them. We did not want to work without the opportunity of getting paid. Because the buyers have to list their home sometime, why not now? Why delay the inevitable if they truly want to sell? If their plans changed we would withdraw the listing.

4. Have you met with a lender yet? This question will start the process of determining their ability to purchase. Truly motivated purchasers meet with lenders. If they have not and they have been looking for 6 months, are they motivated buyers? I don't think so.

Next, determine if they have been prequalified or preapproved. There is a world of difference in these terms and buyers don't know the difference. The focus needs to be to get them to meet with your lender. If they meet with your loan office, you will have solidified your position with them.

Determining the time frame and motivation are critical to earning a paycheck now. If a buyer doesn't want to move for 6 months, then realize that your commission check is also at least 6 months away. How many prospects can you afford to work with when your commission is 6 months away? How much time can you invest in someone who will pay you 6 months to a year from now or never perhaps?

Set Up an Appointment

The best way to qualify people is to ask for an appointment. In this one question you can separate the motivated ones from the unmotivated. The people who are unmotivated will fight not to meet with you.

This appointment should be at your office where you have control. Do not set the appointment at a property. The prospect knows that you are serious about creating a relationship and helping him. If he doesn't want to or is not ready, he will avoid the appointment.

Here is a simple, straightforward script for this appointment, which I call the buyer interview:

> In order for me to provide the highest level of service to you and all my clients, we always set up a meeting prior to showing the properties. Would Tuesday or Wednesday be better for you?

Then the big question is, "If we could find the home in the area that you desire, are you prepared to purchase it now?" If you get a favorable response, set an appointment with them to help them find their new home.

The Effective Listing Presentation

The listing presentation is your moment to show a prospective client all that you're worth. With the value of your services and the relationship you hope to have with a client on the line, it's hard to believe that the less said, the better. But it's true—the longer a listing presentation takes, the worse it gets. The client's mind begins to wander, and the agent begins to promise more in marketing and advertising to keep the client's attention and to procure the listing. The commission rate will have a tendency to decrease and the listing price to increase. This will lead to longer marketing, less profit, or eventually, an expired listing. Truly, the longer your presentation goes the weaker it becomes; a short, focused presentation is the one that will speak volumes for you.

Design Your Questions Today

Top-producers have a specific set of questions that they ask. Their success is not based on chance; it is based on a well-designed system. Develop your system today.

Keep It Short

Many speakers and trainers have been teaching agents for years how to do a 2-hour listing presentation. But think about it: In today's busy society, does anyone really want to listen to an agent talk about himself and his company for 2 hours? In the seller's position, after an hour or so, wouldn't you find yourself thinking about what you would rather be doing with your family? Once the owners begin to think about things other than listing their home with you, it becomes very difficult to get them refocused on signing a contract or agreement.

Remember that the length of your listing presentation is critical to your success.

Ask Questions

One key to making the most effective presentation in the shortest amount of time is to ask questions. To be an effective agent, you need to find out the desires and expectations of the prospect. The only way to do this is by asking questions, and one of the biggest mistakes I see agents making is not asking enough of them. The person asking the questions is the one who controls the conversation. Develop a series of questions to help you to stay focused on your presentation. By asking each client similar questions, you will learn to evaluate each client's motivation, compatibility, and expectations. Working with a standard set of questions will also help you to remember to ask all of the necessary questions. You will be able to standardize your presentation and control the time that your presentation takes. Without a standardized presentation based on a set series of questions, you will have a tendency to take listings for too high a price, for too short a term, or with people whose expectations are not compatible with what your skills and experience can offer them.

To be an effective agent, you need to find out the desires and expectations of the prospect. The only way to do this is by asking questions, and one of the biggest mistakes I see agents making is not asking enough of them.

Direct the Presentation to Price

As you gather information from the sellers and present yourself to them, keep in mind that presentations should be directed, first and foremost, to price, rather than to secondary issues such as marketing or advertising. Price is king in real estate; it is the dominant reason a home sells or fails to sell. Our presentations need to accurately reflect this reality. Rather than focusing on marketing, stick with the issue that will really affect the sale of the home. I advocate rolling up your sleeves and getting down to the business of price, sooner rather than later. If you and the seller cannot agree on price, then nothing else you might say is going to make this relationship work; you should politely excuse yourself and move on to the next prospect.

Plug Yourself

Above all, you need to show the clients the benefit of working with you. This is, after all, what the clients will be paying you for. You need to show them how your skills, experience, and strategy will benefit them. They need to know and understand the benefits of your approach to selling their home. Determine a few of the advantages you offer and share them with the listing prospect.

If you create a step-by-step presentation that is well prepared, concise, focused on price, and clear about what your business offers to the client, you will reduce the time you spend on each presentation. You will also see an improvement in the number of listing presentations that lead to signed contracts. And your clients will thank you for demonstrating respect for their time. You may even have a few minutes left over to spend laughing with your new clients at their stories of "the real estate agent who was here for 2 hours doing a listing presentation."

Creating a Dynamic Listing Presentation

The listing presentation is one of the most misunderstood areas of real estate sales. There are as many theories about this presentation as there are licensed agents in North America. Although the listing presentation has been altered dramatically in the last 5 to 10 years, an efficient and professional presentation will enable the agent to control his clients properly. What are the elements of an efficient, professional listing presentation?

Identify the Problem

First, it is necessary to clearly define a purpose for the listing presentation. Now I know that you are thinking, "Of course, the purpose is to take the listing." You would be partially correct. Certainly the objective is to get the contract signed. The true purpose, though, is to identify the clients' problem in an efficient manner and convey to the clients that you are the person who will provide them the best opportunity to solve their problem in the marketplace. That is really the objective of a professional's listing presentation.

The Issue of Price

Two issues must now be resolved. The first issue is identifying the actual problem itself and the actual problem stems from price. Price will fix everything else in the equation. The price is like the known variable in an algebra equation. You need to search for the other potential issues or potential problems, but they all flow through the known issue, price. By lowering the price, you can sell a property with problems like poor condition, poor location, busy street, functionally obsolete, a "buyer's market," or poor marketing. The list of fixable problems is never ending. Price has a direct correlation to all of these issues. These issues or problems may or may not be interconnected, but price is the only guaranteed connection to all of them. Your presentation should be focused on price, so that you will have an opportunity to get a sale rather than just a listing. Both you and your client want the sale. Neither of you just wants the property listed.

Agree on the Problem

The second key issue is to get your client to agree on the problem. This one certainly is the harder of the two issues. You must have agreement with your client about what the problem is before you can proceed. Because the problem is most often price, you must have a mutual agreement on price. The stronger you are regarding the price, the better chance you have of a sale. Many agents will delay the hard reality, hoping it will go away. Deal with it up front rather than 30 days down the road. You must have the integrity to tell the client the truth. "It won't sell for what you want. You need to lower the price." Do not hedge or mince words. Tell the client straight up that it will not sell. Get an agreement with the client on price before you move on. There is no point in continuing if you and the client do not agree on price. You will be wasting your time. I urge you to have the conviction of your skills as an agent to truthfully interpret the market. Be honest. Most agents want the listing and are unwilling to risk losing the listing even though they know the property will not sell for the client's desired price.

> *Get an agreement with the client on price before you move on. There is no point in continuing if you and the client do not agree on price.*

Sell Yourself

Once you have resolved the pricing issue, you are in the home stretch. Your job now is to convey that you are the real estate agent for the job. Brevity is crucial to success in this arena. Most people do not want to listen to someone talk about how great he is at selling homes. Ask specific questions to see what kind of services they are looking for from their real estate agent. Most people will just say, "We want someone who can sell our home." This is the perfect opportunity to demonstrate your confidence and conviction that you are the one for the job. Look them straight in the eyes and tell them your track record of success and ask them if they are looking for an agent of your caliber. If you do not have a track record, sell your company's record. You may even need to sell a little of both. Finally, ask the clients to sign the paperwork.

Trial Closes

This section of your presentation should last less than 10 minutes unless your clients ask a lot of questions. All during this presentation pepper them with trial closures, for instance, "Do you want a lock box or appointment only? Are there times that would be inconvenient to show the home?" If you are concerned about the condition of the property, ask the clients if they could fix certain items. There are a million trial closes; use a few to test the water. Most people will answer them and proceed.

Ask for the Order

When you have set up a few trial closes and you have already agreed on the price, you have arrived at the moment of truth, so simply ask for the order. It does not have to be elaborate, just ask. Here are a few examples: "I think I have all the information I need; can I have your OK in the box" or "Do you believe I can sell your home?" When they say yes, ask them to sign. If they say no, ask them to tell you why and listen to their answer. Once you have heard their answer, address their concern, and ask them for the order again. Do not give up after the first setback. Did you know that the average sale is made after the fifth or sixth customer refusal? Be persistent; do not give up. If you firmly believe that you are the agent for the job, that belief will come through. People want to select winners to sell their homes.

After the Signing

Lastly, once the contract is signed spend a few minutes debriefing the seller. If you have staff, introduce them to the seller. If you have a routine of communication or a system you use that may be unique, fill them in. A few minutes of explanation will save you the frustrated seller's phone call in 30 days. Let them know you care and appreciate the opportunity, and move on to the next appointment.

Keep It Brief

Many agents do not understand the concept of brevity. They have a 2-hour listing presentation. What in the world are they doing for 2 hours? The seller wants to know each agent's version of the problem, how that agent can solve the problem, and which one is the best agent for the job. The seller really does not care about the rest of the presentation. If you want to be the chosen agent, focus on the problem and the solution. Spending endless amounts of time on other matters or past victories will simply weaken your presentation.

A truly dynamic presentation is short and to the point. Do not break your momentum by going too long or not staying focused during the presentation. Stay directed, focused, and solve their problem.

The Listing Appointment Routine

A successful seller's interview or listing presentation starts before you show up at the house. Top-producers have a specific routine they go through before they arrive to obtain a listing. Before you even begin your presentation, follow the five steps below to ensure that you will also obtain more of the listings you seek.

1. Prepare a solid prelisting package. This presentation should give the client a brief overview of who you are and what your track

record is in sales in their market area. It should clearly focus on the benefits of doing business with you rather than with any other agent. This piece should not be the big "Brag Book" that many people used in the 80s and 90s. Sellers in the new millennium are busy. They don't have the time to read 30 pages about how great you are.

If you are new to real estate, your book will need to be focused on your company and the benefits it offers its clients, such as the marketing plans and other services the client can expect from doing business with you. Your track record will be nonexistent in real estate sales, but if you have relevant experience in other sales or customer service, I would share that. Present that information in a clear, concise fashion. You will want to incorporate graphics that show current market trends with regard to amount of inventory, average days on the market, average list price to sales price, and statistics of success by your company.

If you are new to real estate, your book will need to be focused on your company and the benefits it offers its clients, such as the marketing plans and other services the client can expect from doing business with you.

Lastly, your pricing sections should be clear so the client understands the dangers of overpricing her home. The biggest battle you wage is getting a home priced properly by the seller. By starting that discussion early before the appointment you create momentum for discussion at the actual listing appointment. You also have more credibility when you explain to her that the price she wants is too high for the marketplace.

2. Qualify hard before the appointment. Have a specific set of qualifying questions. The goal is to check the clients' level of motivation to sell. You need to know if their desire to sell is greater than their desire to achieve a certain price. You want to know where and why they are moving. You want to know their desired time frame for moving. That information is related to motivation, and motivation and price are intertwined. The higher the motivation, the lower the price the seller will accept. The lower the motivation, the higher the price the seller will want.

In my qualifying I always wanted to know who else they were interviewing. This information really gave me an edge over the other agents. It allowed me to bring or send them multiple listing service data about the agent or firm. It also gave me the ability to compare services. (Please understand that you don't want to say anything to trash the other agent or company. You do want to point out the differences in your approach and track record compared to theirs.) Most sellers think agents are all alike. I was there to show them that I provided the best opportunity in the marketplace for the sellers to achieve a sale on their home.

If you provide a compelling list of benefits over another agent or firm, sellers will select you almost every time. The only way you will lose a listing is to get out-priced or out-commissioned. It never bothered me to get out-priced or out-commissioned. Those kinds of agents won't last long in most markets. When a potential client makes a selection based on those two issues, are they a client you want to do business with? My answer was no. They didn't have enough respect for me, my team, and real estate agents in general to warrant my investment of time, money, and emotional energy.

3. Develop a preappointment routine. Developing a preappointment routine is essential for success in sales. We need to make sure we are taking all the materials necessary to do the job well on the listing appointment. We also need to make sure we are heading out the door in the right mental state.

Since there is a "zone" in basketball and golf, why not in real estate? What are the steps to enable us to enter the zone? We have all been in it at one time or another, such as the day you have a few appointments booked and they all sign the contract smoothly at your price and terms with little effort, or the day you are prospecting and every call seems to end in a AA Lead or an appointment. We have all had days like this. The question is, How do we get more of them?

The first step is to develop a preactivity routine. If you watch professional golfers hit a shot or make a putt, they will do the same things in sequence through the completion of their shot or putt. If something breaks their concentration during the preshot routine, they start all over again. Basketball players at the free throw line do the same thing. They bounce the ball so many times or flex their knees the same way every time they shoot a free throw.

If you developed a preactivity routine before you went on a listing appointment, your results would improve. You should create a checklist and make sure you are following it. Here is an example of a preactivity routine for a listing appointment.

1. Review the Competitive Market Analysis (CMA) for 30 minutes before you leave the office. The CMA is your evaluation and report of the value of the property.
2. Determine the exact price you want the listing at.
3. Practice the objections you expect will come up from the responses they gave to you after you qualified and confirmed the appointment earlier today.
4. Practice your presentation before you leave the office.
5. Select music to listen to in the car that relaxes you and focuses you on your task. Review the presentation again.
6. Take control before you knock on the door.

If you develop a solid preactivity routine, you will find you will enter the zone more frequently and with more intensity. You should also develop a preactivity routine before prospecting, lead follow-up, negotiating of contracts, and so on.

Don't let success be based on chance. Prepare well before the appointment. Great teams win championships in practice. They win them before the big game is played. Preparation is essential for smooth and successful seller interviews. Start your routine today.

> *Great teams win championships in practice. They win them before the big game is played.*

Ask for the Order

If you really want to take your listing presentation to the professional level, there are two things that separate the really high producers from the other agents in the field. The first is that they ask for the order at the end of their presentation, and the second is that they tape their listing presentation (which will be discussed later in this chapter). The best producers ask the client to sign the contract. The very best agents don't leave until they get a contract signed. They continue to work with the client handling the objections and asking for the order until they get it. Many agents fail to ask for the business at the completion of the presentation. You will not get contracts signed unless you ask.

Trial Closes

One technique to help you with asking for the order is inserting trial closes in your listing presentation. These trial closes create agreement on small items before you gain the big commitment of a relationship. The trial closes will help you achieve "yes" momentum. When your clients continue to say yes on the small items, it will be very hard for them to say no at the contract signing. You will also gain confidence as a salesperson, which will make asking for the order at the end easier.

Some trial closes you could use are:

> Do you want an open house this week or would next week be better?
>
> Should we put the For Sale sign on the right side or left side of the driveway?
>
> Would it be better if I took the pictures of your home today or would you prefer I come back tomorrow?

Clients would have to really struggle to say no to these questions, which are designed to give them a choice and either choice is good for you.

Tag lines

When you get ready to close for the contract, another technique is to insert "tag lines" before you ask for the order. A tag line helps build your position as the authority. You hook it or tag it on before you ask your final closing question. If you receive a positive response, it gives you the green light to close. If you receive a red light, you must ask the prospect why.

One of the great tag lines I used was, "Do you believe I can sell your home?" If they said yes, we had nothing more to talk about. I could then begin filling out the contract and ask for the order. If they feel you could get the home sold, you have little else to discuss.

If they answered no, they had given an indication there is a concern as to your ability. You then must follow up by asking them why. "Why do you believe I couldn't sell your home?" They will share with you a reason or two. Your job is then to answer those concerns and ask for the order. The tag line will help you ferret out the bottom line objection and why the client is not moving forward. Using tag lines effectively will enable you to close with greater ease.

The Close

The closing on a listing appointment is a natural ending to a great presentation. We have a tendency to hesitate at the moment that is most crucial. We must be bold and step forward to ask. Try the authorization close: Mr. and Mrs. Seller, if you just OK this right here, we will get started for you right away."

The authorization close has a couple of key components. One is that you ask them to approve the paperwork. It's a much softer way of saying, "Sign here." Their bodies can often tense up when you say the word *sign.*

People like things done right away. They want definite action now for the commitment they made or for the money they have paid.

Another key component is that you tell them you will start right away. People like things done right away. They want definite action now for the commitment they made or for the money they have paid. We live in an instant society where we expect everything right away.

Focus on asking for the order in every presentation you go on. Even when you think you didn't do well, ask for the order. You might be surprised to get the contract signed.

How Effective Is Your Listing Presentation?

What separates the very best producers from the rest is that they tape their listing presentations. They elevate their skills by taping and reviewing their presentations.

Do you know of any sports team that doesn't watch films of itself and its opponents? Athletic teams and individual players are constantly evaluating their performance by viewing videotapes of the game. If you want to be truly professional, you need to take the step to record your presentation, at least on audiotape.

1. Make the commitment to tape your listing presentations.

2. Buy a small cassette recorder that uses regular-size cassettes so you can listen to the tapes in your car.

3. Prepare a statement to inform your clients why you are taping the conversation and how it benefits them. Example:

> Mr. and Mrs. Seller, I am taping our conversation today for two reasons. The first is to help me follow through on each and every item we discuss regarding your desires and our commitments to you regarding the sale of your home. The second is that I am constantly working to improve my skill in selling real estate, just as a golf professional at the top of his game continues to study his swing. My speaking and selling skills are like my golf swing. By working to be the best, I become even better able to serve you, my client.

4. Listen to the tapes! This is the most difficult part. For some of you it will be one of the most painful experiences you have had in some time. The value to your career, however, will be immeasurable. You will identify things that you are doing right. You will also find out a few things that you are doing wrong.

By listening to the tapes, you will increase your confidence because you will know what your strengths are. You will build stronger rapport with your clients because you will know the areas in which you need improvement.

The tape will also reveal where you are wasting time in your presentation. The listing presentation can almost always be more effective if done in less time. No matter how good you are at the listing presentation, you will find that you talk too much and don't ask enough questions.

5. **Evaluate yourself.** Ask these questions:

What are two or three things I did well?

Did I listen to my client's concerns?

How much time did I talk?

How much time did my client talk?

Did I stay on track during the presentation?

What is one area I could improve on?

What did my client get most excited about?

What steps do I need to take to stay on track better?

6. **Give the tape to a mentor or associate who will review it.** Ask for an honest evaluation. Tell your reviewer what to evaluate. Receive the feedback and make the adjustments that are necessary.

It takes a courageous person to tape presentations and review them. There is always a difference between the truth and our perception of the truth. It takes courage to look the truth in the eye and to look for ways to improve.

We Really Make Three Presentations

The old saying that we always make three presentations is a valid one. The first presentation is the one we make on the way to the appointment. Then there is the actual one that counts. Finally, we make the best one on the way home, when we replay the presentation and get a chance to answer the questions we missed and make the best responses. If you tape your presentations, soon your best ones will be made in the moment that counts, in front of the client.

The Buyer Interview

Another key presentation skill is the buyer interview. The buyer interview is the first step in the buying process. It should happen before you run to the computer to find the buyer the right home. You may be competing with two or three other agents for the same buyer. Why compete when you don't have to? Let the other agents in the marketplace compete and waste their time with disloyal buyers. "Top gun" agents invest their time only with people who are loyal and who will buy through them.

Determine the Buyers' Values and Needs

The buyer interview is separated into three sections. The first section is determining their values and needs. You want to find out what their needs are in a home, such as the number of bedrooms and bathrooms and the layout of the home. To be able to best fulfill their needs, you want to obtain all the information about the property they want to own.

Then you will need to find out the values they are attaching to this new home, the why behind the move, the emotions they are using to make the buying decision. We all buy things because they appeal to our emotions. We then rationalize our emotions through logic. To create long-term satisfied clients, a great salesperson makes sure the buyers' emotions are met.

Understand What Level of Service Buyers Are Looking For

You then must understand the benefits they are looking for you to provide. There are some specific beliefs these people have about real estate agents. They want you to provide a certain type of service. You need to know their expectations of service.

When I was in a buyer interview with someone who wanted me to be available at all times including nights and weekends, we had a problem. I needed to know if my service model of being available only at certain times was acceptable. I also needed to know why the buyer felt I needed to be available 24 hours a day, 7 days a week for him. If I could not persuade him that we would be able to provide him with the highest quality of assistance, I would disengage the appointment and refer him to another agent in the office who was willing to provide the service he felt he needed.

Present the Benefits of Your Services

In the second section of the buyer interview present the benefits of the services that you provide for all your buyers. Have these services on a written form for the buyer so you can show him the benefits he would receive from working with you. People make decisions in the selling process based on emotion and the benefits they receive. If you don't show them their specific benefits, they will not buy. Examples of services and benefits:

1. I will enter into the multiple listing service system your requirements for a home. I will be notified any time that a property meets your specific criteria.

2. I will arrange to get you preapproved with a lender. With preapproval, your offer will be stronger because you have the ability to perform. This eliminates the guesswork for the seller. You will also know the maximum dollar amount that you can purchase.

3. I will give you my professional opinion regarding the price, location, and condition of any property that you are considering

purchasing. My opinion of price, location, and condition is detached and less emotional.

4. I will review and explain all the forms that you will be signing, disclosures, disclaimers, rights of recession, and so on. You will have an explanation and reason for every form that you sign.

5. Once we have successfully negotiated a purchase agreement, I will help you select a home inspector. After the inspection, I will review the report with you to determine if any negotiation is needed with the seller regarding the repairs.

6. When the appraisal is completed, I will review it for accuracy.

7. If there are any lender-required repairs or conditions resulting from the home inspection or appraisal, I will negotiate these items with the seller. I represent you, the purchasers, and your best interests are always my number one concern.

8. Prior to signing all the closing documents, I will review them for accuracy and determine if all the conditions of the purchase agreement have been met. This will protect you from any last-minute surprises and ensure a smooth closing.

The last service listed acknowledges the fact that the seller actually pays our fee. The buyer would receive all these services and benefits free of charge. We would ask for only one thing from him to receive all of these services: his commitment to work with us *exclusively*.

Get the Buyers' Commitment

Next comes section three of the buyer interview. This section I call "The Client Commitment." You don't have a client until he has committed to you. Until then he is only a prospect. This section of the buyer interview separates the "top gun" agent from the rest. You must lay it on the line. He needs to understand that this is your job and how you provide for your family. You owe it to your spouse and children to work only with people who are 100 percent committed to working with you. A buyers' commitment may be something like this:

1. The buyers agree to work with _____ of _____ to find and purchase a home. By working together as a team, purchasers and real estate agent will be able to successfully complete the purchase of a home.

2. If buyers drive by or see an advertisement for a property they are interested in viewing, buyers will call me. I will then obtain all the information regarding the property and set an appointment to view the property. This will eliminate looking at property that doesn't meet the buyers' requirements or needs. Also, I will be able to obtain complete information about the property.

3. In order to conduct my business as a business, my business hours are from _____ to _____. In an emergency, I will return your call within 1 hour, when possible.

4. Buyers will contact me if they see a property that is For Sale By Owner that they are interested in viewing. I will contact the owner and obtain all the information about the property and set an appointment to view the property. Many properties that are For Sale By Owner are willing to work with a real estate agent.

5. Buyers are to be prepared to make an offer when we have found the "right" property.

Real estate is how I make a living; it is my business, my only business. My commitment to you is to do the best job I possibly can through finding the "right" property and by making your buying experience as pleasant as possible.

It's About Commitment

You can provide a high level of service to only a selected number of clients at a time. You cannot help them all. Make sure they want to be helped by you. If they cannot give you a commitment, thank them and refer them to someone else. Invest your time finding another person who will commit. It's all about commitment; either you are or you aren't. "Top gun" agents ask for the commitment, and if they don't get it, they will move on to the next prospect.

Because you are providing all these services for no cost to anyone till closing, you have to ensure that a closing will happen. Draw the buyer in by putting his job in that position. He wouldn't work for a month hoping his paycheck wouldn't bounce at the end of the month. He would find another job.

Objections

Objections are a real part of sales. An objection is that statement or question that stalls that sale temporarily at the moment before you get the contract signed. When most agents hear an objection in the sales process, they often react like deer caught in the headlights: They freeze in terror, moving only at the last second before the buyer or seller runs them over. It doesn't have to be that way.

Often agents view an objection as a big wall between them and the sale, a wall so formidable they can see no way around, over, under, or through. But objections are really like a two-to-three-foot-high picket fence. They have lots of openings. You can climb over them or walk down the fence's length and find the gate. We all want the people to whom we are trying to sell a home to just "roll over and buy." Even a neophyte agent finds it easy to make this type of sale.

Objections Are Opportunities

An unskilled salesperson fears hearing an objection, but a great salesperson views objections as opportunities. Your mental approach to an objection will determine your success or failure. You have to want to love objections. You have to view objections as opportunities to make the sale. In the end, there are no sales without objections.

Objections in the selling process indicate interest. If your clients have no objection, they have no interest in your services. We have to adjust our mindset so that objections are seen as wonderful. The objection lets you know you are less than a couple of steps away from making the sale. Your ability to handle the objection or solve the problem will put you at the doorstep of making the sale.

There are many real estate sales trainers who claim they have invented the objection-free system. The truth is it doesn't exist, even if you are working 100 percent referral- or past client–generated business. You will get asked to cut your commission. They will tell you "I want to think it over." They will explain to you how "the other agent will list our home for a higher price." We all need to be prepared to handle these objections with focus, conviction, and intensity.

Objections give you the opportunity to close for the sale. If you handle the "Will you cut your commission?" objection, you then get to ask for the order. You could say, "Because we have resolved the last issue, do you want me to handle the sale for you?" Always follow up your objection-handling techniques with a closing question or tag line. You want to go on the offensive right away. You are playing defense in objection handling, but it can change to offense in a second. Make sure you take advantage of this opportunity.

Listen Carefully

When you get an objection from buyers or sellers, make sure you hear clearly what they are saying. If you interpret the objection incorrectly, the answer you give, no matter how eloquent, will not be sufficient to overcome their area of concern.

Let me give you a few techniques I have used to turn objections into dollars. I would pause to make sure I clearly understood and then repeated what they said or asked them to explain further. This technique would do a few things for me. When I confirmed what their objection was to ensure I had understood it, I bought myself a few seconds to prepare an answer. I was able to respond in a powerful, well-planned manner. I would avoid the big mistake of trying to answer the objection before the buyer or seller gets the objection out of her mouth, as if stopping her from stating the objection completely would stop the objection. The objection is legitimate to that person, no matter how ridiculous it may sound. She feels it is legitimate; therefore it is! Interrupting can cause the seller or buyer to become irritated with you. It may not matter how well you handle the objection if you interrupt.

There Is a Limited Amount of Objections

Most agents dread hearing an objection, but most objections result from one of two situations. The first situation occurs because the seller or buyer has legitimate concerns regarding the property or your skills to sell her home.

The other situation arises because your presentation was not good enough. You did not convey the confidence that you are the person for the seller to hire for the sale of her home; you did not make a convincing enough presentation for the buyer to purchase the home you showed her. The client's desire to work with you is a natural ending to a good presentation. If the presentation is weak, the objections will flow like a river.

There are really only about 40 possible objections in the selling of real estate. If you wrote them all down and practiced them for half an hour a day for the next 6 months, you would know them automatically. You would be prepared for any situation in selling. You would then have the confidence to say, "Bring them on; I am ready for

Practice Objection Handling

NFL teams spend 4 to 6 hours a day practicing football. The players and coaches spend a couple more hours a day reviewing film and studying their play books during a 2-month span in spring training; then they play four practice games in preseason to prepare for the real NFL season. During the season the players and coaches spend a few hours a day practicing and watching films 5 or 6 days a week to prepare for *one* 60-minute game. They will spend 40 to 50 more times practicing and preparing for the game than actually playing the game. How skilled in sales would you be if you adopted that regimen? How about if you practiced even 1 hour a day on your skills at overcoming objections? You would become an unstoppable real estate salesperson.

them." About 10 to 15 of the most common objections will stop unprepared agents in their tracks 90 percent of the time. How difficult would it be to learn just those 10 objections in the next 30 to 60 days?

Solve the Problem, Then Close

Objections are an opportunity to get a signed contract. When a buyer or seller gives you an objection, he is presenting you with the opportunity to close. He is basically saying, "I like this, but there is one factor I do not like." The buyer might say, "If the home you are showing me had a larger patio, it would be right for me." All you have to do is get him a larger patio and you have made a sale! You must put your problem-solver hat on. If you solve his problem, then you get the opportunity to ask him to buy. The client can say yes or give you another objection. If he gives you another objection, you get another opportunity to solve the problem and ask him to buy. This procedure may continue for a few objections. Do not give up; you are getting closer to a sale. As long as you are able to continue to solve his problem, the client will buy. Remember, you are the problem solver.

What to Do About Price Objections

When the seller feels that her home is worth more than the marketplace or more than you would recommend, this is your signal to go back to the price. Reemphasize the importance of proper pricing. Show her that she will be the highest bidder for her home. Remove the emotion from the discussion and look at the facts. The more emotion you allow into the discussion, the higher the price the seller will want. You must have conviction and belief in your price. Remember this is your opportunity to overcome the concern and then ask for the order again.

What to Do If a Seller Is Concerned About Your Abilities

If the seller's concern is about your abilities, this objection stems from your presentation and conviction. When this arises the great agents will go back and focus on their track record. They will focus on telling the seller about their ability to get the job done. Once they have done that they will ask for the agreement from the seller. This can be done many ways. I often used a question such as, "Do you believe I can sell your home?" If they said yes, I asked for the order. If they said no, I used the most important and powerful word in sales, why. It allowed me to get to the bottom line of the objection.

The Most Common Objections

There are about 40 possible objections you will encounter in real estate. You can learn to counter them all. The most common are:

> Will you cut your commission?
>
> I want to think it over.
>
> The other agent will cut his commission.
>
> The other agent will list my home for more money.
>
> We want a shorter listing term.

If you learn to handle these few you will be far ahead of your competition. I have found that even 10-year veteran agents struggle with these on a daily basis. You can be better than they are in a short time by mastering this process.

Let me share with you how to handle each of these objections:

1. Will you cut your commission? "I realize that you are trying to save money. I can appreciate that. Which of the services do you want me to cut out of the marketing of your home? Or do you want our full marketing program?"

2. I want to think it over. "I agree that evaluating a decision is important. If you had to make a decision right now, whether to list with me or not, what would you decide? Why don't we go ahead? Do you realize it takes a week to 10 days to alert the world you are for sale? Can we really afford to wait?"

3. The other agent will cut his commission. "Mr. Seller, I realize you can get someone to list your home for a lesser fee. Here is my concern for you . . . if they can't even negotiate their own brokerage fee, how can they negotiate a good sale price for your home. When they are not skilled enough to protect their money, how quickly will they try to give away yours?"

4. The other agent will list my home for more money. "I can understand why you would be led in that direction. Here is the truth. A lot of agents will tell you anything you want to hear just to get your listing. Are you just interested in having your property listed or are you truly interested in getting sold? The question that you have to answer is, Who can get your home sold? Do you think I can get your home sold?"

5. We want a shorter listing term. "I can understand how you feel. The truth is, in our market today, it often takes 3 to 6 months to get a home sold. Did you know that? Do we need to list your home tonight at 10 to 20 percent below fair market value to ensure a sale within your shorter listing period? Then we will keep the longer listing period of 6 months. Will that work for you?"

Objections allow you to have the success you want in your sales career. Don't be like most agents who fear and avoid them. Resolve to practice and meet them head on.

Your sales skills will dictate your level of success in real estate sales. You must develop a game plan to increase your sales skills today. What are you waiting for?

"We are all paid in life based on our ability to sell."

—Earl Nightingale

Making Good Things Happen

One of the best things about being in real estate sales is there are no limits. There are no limits as to the money you can earn. There are no limits as to the investments you can own and control. There are no limits as to the time off you take. However, as a brand new agent, you can often feel like there are limits on you every time you turn around. The truth is there are no limits on your earnings in your first year. I have seen agents make $100,000 and beyond in their first year in the business. If another person has done it, so can you! In this chapter we discuss some practical things you can do to accomplish your goals.

Where Will You Be in 5 Years?

The biggest limit we set is our undefined outcome, which occurs because we don't have goals for what we want to accomplish. Well-defined and well-set goals allow us to go beyond where others are today. When President Kennedy set the goal in the early 60s that in the following 10 years we would be placing a man on the moon, everyone thought he was crazy. We were nowhere close to accomplishing that feat. Miraculously, within that 10-year span, Neil Armstrong made that small step for man and that giant leap for mankind. Man walked on the moon because it was a goal that was focused on and embraced by many. Your goals will have that same power in your life. In 5 years you will end up somewhere—the question is, where. The decision where you end up is up to you. In 5 years you will have a certain lifestyle. The question is, What will it be? That decision is yours.

In 5 years you will end up somewhere—the question is, where. The decision where you end up is up to you.

Take 15 Minutes to Dream

What do you want in the next 5 years? I am going to help you find out with this exercise. Get a piece of paper right now. This is the most important decision you will make this year. Take 15 minutes to write down at least 50 important things you want. Let me give you a couple of hints:

1. What do you want to earn?
2. What do you want to own?
3. Where do you want to travel?
4. What do you want to become?
5. What do you want to learn?

Write as fast as you can. Keep your mind free-flowing. Don't limit yourself. Don't allow the negative voice to say, "You can't have that!" Put this book down right now and make the list!

Select Your Top Goals

Now that you have your list, let's review it. Next to each item write the number of years you think it will take you to achieve it. For example, if you wrote that you want a blue Porsche Boxster, and it will take you 3 years to get one, put the number three by it. If you wrote $100,000 income and you believe you can do it in 1 year, write

The Power Source Behind Goals

If your desire to earn $100,000 was tied to a great enough reason why, you will accomplish that goal. If you are a parent and one of your children had to have a $100,000 operation and there was no other way to raise the money but sell a lot of homes, would you make that $100,000? I don't know too many parents who wouldn't find a way around the roadblocks to make the money needed for their child. The "why" behind the goal is ultimately the power source. It's the power source that pulls you toward the accomplishment of the goals.

One of my goals in real estate was to make $100,000 my first full year. My "why" was my passion for financial independence and early retirement. My father retired at 57 from dentistry. I wanted to make sure I did it much earlier than that. I had something to prove. I entered real estate on a mission of wealth. The fire of that passion got fanned by the agents in my office. They were experienced and they often laughed at my coming in at 7:00 A.M. to set up my day and begin prospecting at 8:00 A.M. They felt what I was doing was a waste of time.

I resolved then to show them by becoming the top agent in my office and fulfill the prophecy of the old saying, "Massive success is your best revenge." Maybe there is someone who said to you, at one time, that you couldn't do it or that you would never amount to anything. Here is your chance to create the success you want and to have the life you want.

the number one. Repeat this process for each item that you have written down.

Now select the three top 1-year, 3-year, and 5-year goals. Then write a paragraph on each of these goals describing the reason you want to achieve this specific goal. For instance, you may want to know how it feels to possess and drive a Boxster or what it will feels like to be a millionaire. You must have strong and compelling reasons why you want to accomplish these goals.

Although the written goals will not remove all the roadblocks to your success, they will make you resolve to discipline yourself to meet or exceed them.

Although the written goals will not remove all the roadblocks to your success, they will make you resolve to discipline yourself to meet or exceed them. When there is something we truly desire, we find a way to obtain it. What you want is a huge motivator only when it is linked to the compelling reason why you want it.

Make $100,000 in Your First Year

Here is a plan for making $100,000 in your first year in the real estate business. This plan, if followed every day for 240 workdays this year, will make $100,000 for you, provided you work 20 days per month.

Goal	$100,000
Yearly Income	$100,000
Quarterly Income	$ 25,000
Monthly Income	$8,333
Weekly Income	$2,083
Daily Income	$416

The average gross commission check for most markets is $3,500. Let's figure out the number of homes you need to sell:

Goal	$100,000	
Yearly Income	$100,000	29 homes
Quarterly Income	$25,000	7 homes
Monthly Income	$8,333	2.5 homes
Weekly Income	$2,083	.625 homes

For you to make $100,000 in a year in most markets you need to sell a little over one home every other week. You can take 4 to 5 weeks off during the year and still make your goal of $100,000. You also can work a normal schedule of hours—40 to 50 hours a week. The key is focusing on the activities that pay you the most money. For you to make $100,000 working 45 hours a week and only 48 weeks a year, you have to focus your time.

Value of time equation: 48 weeks x 45 hours a week = 2160 total hours worked

$100,000 / 2160 = $46.00 per hour

Your Step-by-Step Plan

Here is your plan for earning $100,000 your first year in real estate:

1. Be at the office early. No later than 8:00 A.M. Most agents don't show up until the day is half over. Your day should start no later than 8:00. You have the opportunity to get a lot accomplished before everyone else starts to distract you. Your broker will also be impressed with your commitment to excellence.

2. Start working on your sphere of influence. These are all the people you know. Your main job the first week is to construct a database of people you know or could know. First, write down all the

Your main job the first week is to construct a database of people you know or could know.

areas of your life on the form we have provided at the end of the chapter (see Figure 1). If you are involved in a church, a bowling league, your spouse's work, or your children's athletic teams, write them all down—as many areas as possible. Don't forget your old job. List people you know who play key roles in your life. These might include brothers, sisters, or parents. All these people know other people. And remember that studies have shown that most people know at least 250 other people.

Once you have all the areas of your life defined, list all the people you know from each area. You can use the form we have included at the end of this chapter (Figure 2). If you don't know all the information, you will need to research it. If you are missing an address and they have the phone number, call your future clients and ask for it. If you have the address and no phone number or no address at all, you have a couple of options. You can get your title company to do the research if you work in a state that has title companies. Ask them to search a certain address or even a specific name for phone numbers. They will see if the phone number is on the county records. You could also go to a crisscross directory. This directory is usually arranged by streets and addresses and also by names. You can often pick up phone numbers that way. You can also do a search for people on the Yahoo! Web site (www.yahoo.com). You need to have complete information for all your spheres of influence. Your job this first week is to get as many people as possible in your sphere right away. You will continue to add people every week (Figure 3). Remember, however, that in order to get your career off to a great start you need as many people as possible in the first week.

If you are going to use a computer database, such as Top Producer, ACT!, or Online Agent, your objective is to get all your names in that database this week. If you are not skilled at typing, hire someone to input the data into the program. You must get this done in the first week. I meet agents regularly who have been in the business for 10, 15, even 20 years and they have never done this. Do you want to be like one of them a few years down the road?

3. Study the marketplace. It's imperative that you know the marketplace. In the end, it doesn't matter whether you are in a good market or bad one. It's the one you are in and it may not change. You have to know the marketplace statistics so you can react properly to the marketplace. However, it's not the marketplace that has the greatest effect on your income; it's what you do with the marketplace you are in that matters. If you make a career of real estate sales, you will experience both good and bad markets. Knowledge of trends in the marketplace helps you react appropriately.

Your job in week one is to know the multiple listing service statistics for the board and, specifically, for your company. Use the form "Statistics You Must Know"(Figure 4) found at the end of this chapter to help you. You will also want to look at the numbers for at least 3 to 4 months prior to the start of your sales career. You need to memorize these statistics so you can insert them into your conversation with prospects, clients (both buyers and sellers), and other agents. This activity must be done monthly so you are ahead of the market trends. You can receive this data from the multiple listing service. If you are having difficulty finding this information, talk with your broker.

These statistics will also give you power when you go in for listing appointments and buyer interviews. If your company's average list price to sale price is higher than the board, you will be able to show the seller you will make her more money. If you see the actual number of homes coming on the market increasing, while the number of sales is staying constant, you will be able to counsel your seller that price is a big issue, because buyers have more to choose from now than 60 days ago. You become much more of an expert because you have researched the trends of your marketplace.

4. Preview property. To really know and understand the marketplace, we need to preview homes. We need to see what someone can buy for a specific amount of money in the areas in which we work. We need to know what someone can buy for $100K, $150K, $200K, $250K, and all the way to the upper ranges of the marketplace.

A new agent should preview at least 15 homes a week. This preview process must continue for 6 months. At the end of 6 months you will have seen enough properties to not have to do it daily. You might want to preview once or twice a month to keep up on the inventory.

> *A new agent should preview at least 15 homes a week.*

When working with buyers you should preview all the homes that you plan to show them. This allows you to be prepared before you enter the home. It shows the buyers that you are knowledgeable about the marketplace and the homes in their price range. When you preview, you will not be embarrassed by showing a home that is substandard. You can cross that home off before you show it.

5. Take top agents to lunch. You can learn a great deal from other agents who are successful. They can share with you how they got to the top. The top agents in your office have gotten where they are for a few specific reasons. You need to find out what they are. Here is a list of questions to ask them:

What are the three least effective things you see new agents do?

What three things did you do early in your career that made you successful?

What were the three big mistakes you made early in your career?

If you were starting over tomorrow, what are the three things you would do?

What are the biggest time wasters in our business?

What one skill do I need to acquire to be successful right away?

What do you see our market doing in the next 6 months, 1 year, and 3 years?

Is there anything I can do for you for taking the time to meet with me?

May I ask you for advice from time to time?

6. Write 10 personal notes a day. The personal, handwritten note is one of the most powerful tools in selling. For decades it has been the staple of great salespeople in terms of time and involvement and in importance to the receiver. Most salespeople do not send personal notes. They don't take the time for that type of correspondence. We need to make the time because it will prove to be time and money well spent.

If you receive vast amounts of junk mail as I do, you probably sort it all right over the garbage can. I am very quick to throw out everything that is unnecessary. I then arrange the real mail. The bills and other letters that are in those #10 envelopes go in one pile. Then I see that wonderful invitation-size envelope. I get excited and open that one first. The way to really get noticed is to send personal notes. They are even more important today because most communication is by e-mail. People who are in business use e-mail heavily because of the instant communication and the cost . . . free! That is why a handwritten note today has more power than ever before. It is uncommon, so make sure you send out 10 every day.

Send notes to people who provide you service. Send them to your sphere and past clients. Send them to people who call about a property. There is no limit to whom you can send a note.

Here are a few sample starts and finishes to personal notes:

1. I don't know the last time I said thanks, but thanks!
2. I tried to call you today; unfortunately I missed you. I needed to tell you . . .
3. I was thinking of you today and ran across this information. I thought you might find it helpful. (Send quote, property, news article, and so on.)
4. Thank you for taking the time today. I know that you are very busy so any time you spend is valuable.
5. I wanted to personally thank you for the referral of _____. It is a delight to have clients like you.
6. Thank you for the referral of _____. Being recommended by you means a lot to me.
7. I was reviewing my (files, database, sphere) and realized it's been too long since . . .
8. I found myself thinking about you today, so I thought I would write you a quick note.

The system for notes is very simple: Write notes that have three to five lines. Notes should be short and to the point. Use a broad-tipped pen; don't use a regular ballpoint. Use a medium roller ball or better. You want the note to be bold in its appearance. Use a unique close on the note or a call to action. Set yourself apart by sharing something you have that is a unique opportunity. Hit the minimum standard of 10 per day, every day. Don't fail even one day to do this. This is one of the most effective marketing strategies you can use. It is easy to do and inexpensive. When you are a new agent, often your company will pay for note cards and postage, so it's free. Don't fail to embrace this personal way to market yourself.

7. Mail announcement cards or letters to your sphere. You need to announce to everyone you know that you are in business. They need to know that you are ready to serve them. You also want to ask for referrals from them. The referrals from your sphere can be the lifeblood of your business. You are either going to have to contact people you know or people you don't know: Which is easier to do?

You need to announce to everyone you know that you are in business. They need to know that you are ready to serve them. You also want to ask for referrals from them.

8. Spend at least an hour a day in personal development. The keys to success for any agent are knowledge and the control of time. Your ability to acquire the knowledge and skill now will dictate how quickly you become a success. The hour you invest daily into practicing scripts and dialogues or reading and studying success will be immeasurably more valuable than talking at the water cooler. Don't neglect to work to improve your skills daily.

You want to repeat these steps each week for your first year or until you get eight listings. Then you can drop the preview property step from daily to weekly. There is one other activity you want to add starting in week two and continuing throughout the rest of your sales career.

9. Prospect daily a set amount of contacts. As a new agent, you should start with a minimum of five contacts per day. A contact means actually talking to people who could buy or sell or refer you to someone who could. Your job starting in week two is to call all the people in your sphere. By working to grow your sphere, you will be able to make more sphere calls and less cold calls. You can also

Create Financial Independence

If you apply the system we've outlined, you will be successful. The daily activities you do will create the success that you desire. Start each day with the focus to do these nine steps before the week is complete. One of the best things about being a real estate salesperson is the money you can earn. This profession, done well, can create your financial independence. It can give you the tools to achieve the American dream of homeownership, a large income, investments, and nice vehicles. It is all there for you.

call your sphere again every quarter. Gradually you will want and need to raise your contact total to 10 per day. The most successful agents in the country prospect regularly. Start the habit of picking up the phone to generate revenue daily right now.

My Father's Advice

Most people I know who decide to sell real estate do it because they think they can make a lot of money. They have a passion to earn a high income. They want to earn six figures and beyond. If I am describing you, let me give you some wise counsel. It was the same counsel I received many years ago from my father. He shared with me that his dental practice provided the cash flow that allowed him to make other investments. These other investments were the vehicles that created the wealth in the end. These other investments allowed him to retire at an early age. Dentistry provided the steady income and savings that allowed him to borrow for real estate investments he made and the capital stocks he bought.

The most successful agents in the country prospect regularly. Start the habit of picking up the phone to generate revenue daily right now.

When I entered real estate I viewed my real estate sales business the same way he viewed his dental practice. It's the business that generates the cash flow that allows you to achieve your definition of financial independence. My real estate business allowed me to fund a retirement account annually, buy investment property, develop land into lots, build houses for resale, and make a number of other investments. Your career can do the same for you. You can create the life and wealth that you have always desired. Apply a few simple rules and you can achieve the financial position you want in life.

Poor Preparation for Financial Independence

Even when agents make more than a six-figure income, the vast majority have not dramatically improved their financial balance sheet. After looking at hundreds of agents' P&L (Profit and Loss) statements and personal spending habits, I've determined that real estate agents are poorly prepared for financial independence. Why should real estate agents be any different from the American population in general?

According to the Social Security Administration, of 1000 randomly selected people from age 25 to age 65, statistics indicate:

- 190 are dead—19 %
- 150 have incomes more than $30,000—15 %
- 660 have incomes of less than $30,000—66%

Let's look at these numbers. There are more people deceased than earning something close to a decent quality of life. Of the people still alive, 66 percent of them exist on less than $30,000 per year. My question is: Which group do you want to be in? Which group are you heading for based on your financial plan, investment choices, and savings plan?

Reasons for Financial Failure

These are the top three reasons people fail in their finances:

- They never create a financial plan.
- They make poor investment choices.
- They put off starting a savings plan.

Let me share with you a few simple rules that will ensure that you don't join the 66 percent earning less than $30,000. I have used these rules with hundreds of agents to transform their financial picture in a short period of time.

Rule 1: Track Your Expenses Both Business and Personal

You must know where the money is going. Separate your business from personal expenses. Establish a business checking account and pay all business bills through it. Too many agents mingle their business commission checks and business bills with personal and household expenses. It is more difficult to control your money when you can't track it. Enter all your expenses and revenue in an accounting software program. I think the easiest is Quicken. Quicken will allow you to accurately track your cost to run the business; then you can run a monthly P&L statement to see where you are spending your money. The money you earn in real estate can come in bunches. It can be very easy to spend that large commission check that's burning a hole in your pocket.

Separate your business from personal expenses. Establish a business checking account and pay all business bills through it.

When we have money, a want looks like a need because we have the ability to buy it. We begin to rationalize our wants into needs. For most of us a want that our neighbor already owns becomes a need.

Rule 2: Adjust Your Lifestyle

Spending less than you earn makes up 90 percent of financial planning. The premise involves saving money and making sacrifices. The ability to pay now in the form of adjusted lifestyle and saving the difference will allow you to play later. To play later you will need more than $30,000 per year. Thomas Stanley, who wrote the book, *The Millionaire Next Door,* summed up how the vast majority accumulated their millions: "They lived well below their means." Living beyond our means is a national epidemic. Consumer credit card debt in the United States is in excess of $528 billion. Roughly two-thirds of Americans who have credit cards do not pay off their monthly balance. We are clearly living beyond our means. Take a close look at your monthly obligations and evaluate where you are spending your money.

Rule 3: Aggressively Reduce Your Debt

There is an old proverb that speaks of a borrower being a servant to the lender. The weight and pressure of debt can be crippling. I have seen this happen to agents for years. I have even seen it manifested in my own life. I have not always made the wisest choices with my money. Fortunately, I have made more wise choices than foolish ones.

If you have credit card debts, make a decision to pay them off. Start with the credit card with the highest interest rate first. Decide on a monthly amount that you can commit to reducing your debt. If you stretch, you will be able to find a few hundred dollars per month to pay toward your debt. Most credit card companies require you to pay 2 percent of the balance owed monthly. Let's look at that practice. Let's say you have a debt of $2,705 with an interest rate of 18.38 percent. Your 2 percent toward the outstanding balance would take you 27 years, 2 months to pay it off. You would pay $11,047 in total interest. How do you feel about eating out more often now? If you increased your payment to 8 percent or to $216.40 per month, it would take 2 years, 1 month to pay it off. You would pay $94 in interest. You need to accelerate your payments to reduce your debt. You must adopt a cash mentality. This cash mentality will allow you to charge only what you have funds to pay for.

Rule 4: Create a Savings Plan Now

The biggest enemy in financial planning is procrastination. People wait too long to start saving. The truth is, becoming a millionaire is not very difficult. The power of compounding interest will take care of your needs. According to *Investors Business Daily*, a 20-year-old person needs to invest only $1,014 per year or $2.78 per day with an annual return of 11 percent to have $1 million saved by the age of 65. Look at the daily number of $2.78. Who couldn't save that amount per day, even at the age of 20? Even someone working for minimum wage could do that with ease. My mentor, Jim Rohn, used to say, "What is easy to do is also easy not to do." It's easy to save the $2.78, but it's also easy to buy a latte every day at Starbucks instead of saving. That's all we are talking about here—choosing financial independence planning rather than the latte.

You must adopt a cash mentality. This cash mentality will allow you to charge only what you have funds to pay for.

Therefore, we need to create a system that automatically removes the money when we receive it. We need to transform ourselves into savers. We are not a nation of savers although we really need to be. Savers pay themselves first. It's amazing how little you miss money that never comes into your possession. On average, Americans save less than 5 percent of their disposable income. Let's compare the United States to other countries in regard to income saved:

Germans are saving	11.5%
Japanese are saving	12.2%
Belgians are saving	17.0%

We are behind in our need to pay our savings accounts first.

The secret to saving is writing the check to savings first. Do it before paying other bills and obligations. Saving is a habit to be forged. Here is the formula I used on each of my commission checks for many years:

20%	went to a tax account
10%	went to a retirement savings account
10%	went to a business savings account

These percentages ensured that my taxes were always current and my retirement account was always fully funded. There were also reserves for an investment opportunity or a slow closing month. The more you make your money disappear into protected accounts, the more you will have for later.

Pay Now or Pay Later

Creating financial wealth is the process of being diligent with your money. I remember some Fram oil filter commercials that were a lot like creating financial independence. The service station attendant, while looking under the hood of the car, was trying to convince the customer to use a Fram oil filter. The premise was that the quality of the Fram filter was better for his engine than the bargain brand. He said to the customer, "You can pay me now or pay me later." He was implying that the customer could spend a few more dollars now for the Fram oil filter or get the cheaper brand and have his engine rebuilt later. The same is true with your money. You will have to pay either way. The price you pay now is small compared to the price you will have to pay later if you are not diligent in managing your money and financial affairs. Which price do you want to pay?

Figure 1. Spheres of Your Life

_____	_____
_____	_____
_____	_____
_____	_____
_____	_____
_____	
_____	_____
_____	_____
_____	_____
_____	_____
_____	_____

Figure 2. Sphere of Influence

Name	Address	Phone	Relationship
_____	_____	_____	_____
_____	_____	_____	_____
_____	_____	_____	_____
_____	_____	_____	_____
_____	_____	_____	_____
_____	_____	_____	_____
_____	_____	_____	_____
_____	_____	_____	_____
_____	_____	_____	_____
_____	_____	_____	_____
_____	_____	_____	_____
_____	_____	_____	_____
_____	_____	_____	_____
_____	_____	_____	_____
_____	_____	_____	_____
_____	_____	_____	_____
_____	_____	_____	_____
_____	_____	_____	_____

Figure 3. Names Added to Sphere List

Name	Address	Phone	Circumstance	Note Sent

Figure 4. Statistics You Must Know

	The Board	Your Company
Total active residential listings	_____	_____
Compared to last year at this time	_____	_____
Average list price	_____	_____
Average market time	_____	_____
Compared to last year at this time	_____	_____
List price versus sales price ratio	_____	_____
Compared to last year	_____	_____
Number of sales YTD	_____	_____
Average sales price	_____	_____
Compared to last year	_____	_____
Current interest rate 30-year fixed	_____	_____

Taking Your Career to the Next Level

11

Nobody wants to be a new agent forever. We want to learn, grow, and improve. This chapter will focus on some of the traps to avoid and the steps you must take to achieve your full potential in this business.

How to Avoid Some Common Mistakes

Being successful as a real estate agent demands a wide variety of skills. All too often, the only way to develop these skills is to make mistakes. I was talking to an agent recently who had moved to a smaller town in a more rural area than the big city she had worked in before. She told me how much she had had to learn the hard way about septic systems, wells, and water quality because she had sold only homes on city sewer and city water prior to the move. She described how she had just assumed that the water and sewer services were like her previous marketplace. Her new market was nothing like her old market. She had put her buyer through tremendous stress by the end of the transaction because of her lack of knowledge. She had exposed her buyer to a lower value for the property due to her lack of diligence in checking out the facts regarding the property.

The Louisiana Pacific Fiasco

In Portland, Oregon, where I sold real estate in the 1990s, Louisiana Pacific siding became a significant problem, as it did for real estate agents throughout the United States. Because new homes in the 90s where selling as quickly as builders could put them up, hundreds of thousands of homes were built with LP siding during that time. When you couple that with the rainy climate in Portland, a significant amount of homeowners faced the problem of swelling and deteriorating siding. Added to that was the media frenzy that ensued, causing a panic among both buyers and sellers. As agents we had to be prepared to solve the problem for our clients; we have to be knowledgeable enough to help them evaluate their options and guide them to the best decision.

Never Assume

One of the first rules in real estate is to never assume. Take the time to verify the information if you have any doubt. For example, it was easier for this agent to take the sellers' word that they are on a sewer line instead of on a cesspool. Make sure you educate yourself on the different options of water supply and waste removal relative to a particular property. Be sure that you have a working knowledge of the types of roofs that are on homes in your marketplace and the longevity of the different types. Be able to recognize the different types of exterior siding applied to homes in your marketplace.

Acquiring knowledge is an essential step in taking your career to the next level. To take your career to the highest level you need to master your knowledge of real estate and real property. There are always areas of mastery that require our time and resources to learn.

Read These!

When I entered real estate at age 28, I learned of a new arena of education—personal development. I had never heard of Earl Nightingale, Napoleon Hill, Zig Ziglar, Tom Hopkins, Les Brown, Jim Rohn, Brian Tracy, and many others. I was unaware that there were resources out there in the form of audiocassettes, seminars, and books that could allow me to dramatically raise my thinking, skills, and income.

I remember attending my first Jim Rohn seminar where he dared all of us to spend as much time working on ourselves as we did on our jobs. Then he challenged us to buy and read two specific books. One was *Think and Grow Rich* by Napoleon Hill. The other was *The Richest Man in Babylon* by George Clason. Jim predicted that I needed to get both those books in the next 24 hours or I would never get them. He focused on causing action to happen right now. We often have good intentions, but those feelings will quickly fade. In life you have to act when the emotions are high. You must act when the intent is most passionate. I purchased both those books that very evening on the way home from the seminar. My total investment was around $12, but what a small amount it proved to be.

Don't Wait, Do It Now

I give you the same challenge today that Jim Rohn gave me 12 years ago: Go out and get those two books today! Don't wait until tomorrow; do it now. Those books will change your life. They will lead you as they have me down the path to other books, audiocassette tapes, CDs, and seminars. Their messages will expand your thoughts, beliefs, and actions.

In the final analysis, we don't get paid for the knowledge we possess; we get paid for the knowledge we *apply*. We are paid for action. Bring the ideas in these two books into action. They will be the catalysts for you to walk the path of personal development. Your ability to continually invest in yourself will bring you the greatest return on your investment and will bring returns far greater than the stock market or real estate investments. The objective is to invest in yourself.

The Four Paths

As a real estate agent, there are several paths you can take to get to the next level in your career. I have identified four paths that people take to reach the top level of success in the real estate field. You will use one of these trails to achieve "top gun" status, but you must expect to pay a price for whichever path you choose.

Become a Workaholic

The most common path is to become a workaholic. This path causes you to trade large amounts of time for the amount of income that is created. Workaholic agents toil 6 to 7 days a week to achieve their goals. They never get off the treadmill of client control, lack of respect by clients and prospects, uncertainty as to where their income will come from, and putting their career before their family. This path forces us to focus only on the result of earning a specific amount of money, regardless of the consequences. The process or journey along the way is of little value because the goal is income.

The finish line of maximized income is all that matters. The vast majority of high gross commission agents have taken this path to the top. They have paid the price in missed tee-ball games, piano recitals, and date nights with their spouse. Still, this is the most common route to financial success for agents.

Buy Your Way to the Top

This technique is the second most popular that agents use to reach the top. There are really two different ways agents buy their way to the top: They do it through reduction in commission or in massive expense in the marketing area. Either way, buying the business eventually catches up with you.

Commission Cutting

If you achieve "top gun" status through commission cutting, it is hard to reverse this trend. When that client comes back a handful of years later, she is going to want the same concessions as before to get the job done. Most of the referrals of friends and family from this source are also going to expect a lowered commission. You will eventually turn your whole business into a discount operation. All your clients will expect the 5 percent charge that you gave to all the others. Don't be naïve in thinking that no one will know. The word will get around. The lowering of commission substantially reduces your gross revenue and your net profit. It may not seem like much when you look at one transaction, but when you look at the whole year or a whole career, it's a monstrous number.

The workaholic path causes you to trade large amounts time for the amount of income that is created.

    Let me give you an example: You decide to list a home for 5 percent rather than 6 percent. It's a $200,000 home in a terrific neighborhood in your market—the kind of listing everyone wants. Instead of getting $6,000, you receive only $4,000. Your broker takes his 50 percent split and you are left with $2,000 for your effort. You are happy you did the deal because you made $2,000. If you did four more transactions this quarter with these exact circumstances, you would be short $10,000 in gross commission income (GCI). After the company split, you would have lost $5,000 out of your own pocket. Repeat that process for a full year and you lose $40,000 in GCI and $20,000 income to you after your company split. If you repeat this for your career of 10 years, you have lost more than $400,000 in gross commissions. You have also lost at least $200,000 in real dollars of income for yourself.

Buying the business through reduction of commission is very expensive. I realize that it doesn't seem like much on one deal, but it adds up quickly. I was coaching an agent a year ago and had him add up all the commissions he gave away. He called me the next day and was physically sick because of the lost revenue. He had given away more than $50,000 that year in commission. Reducing your commission causes future havoc for yourself, your company, and your clients.

> *Buying the business through reduction of commission is very expensive.*

Some of our clients and their properties are going to demand more of our time and energy and advertising dollars. If we reduce our commissions on the easy transactions, then all we have left are the difficult ones that require more time and energy to complete and close. Most clients at this time want a fixed price for your services. They want to know what you are going to charge. They are not willing to take the risk as to whether their home sells or not. Your objective is to fix your commission price and hold firm. Don't back down when someone asks, "Will you cut your commission?"

Massive Marketing

The other way many agents buy the business is massive advertising and marketing. This no-holds-barred, spend-money-to-make-money strategy always spells trouble. Anyone can attract more business by spending money in advertising, but we often get sucked into what I call the one-for-one trade: an ad or mailer that produces only one deal. Ads or mailers can cost us about what we would generate in one transaction. We feel good that we generated a deal, but we don't count the cost of generation. We must avoid the one-for-one trade.

If I were going to advertise and market for additional business, my rule is a minimum tenfold return for the dollars and labor spent to produce the revenue.

If I were going to advertise and market for additional business, my rule is a minimum tenfold return for the dollars and labor spent to produce the revenue. You need to either prepare the copy or hire someone else to prepare it, and there are real costs for labor associated with creating that marketing campaign. It's easy to get faked out by the one-for-one trade.

Become Unethical

A third way to get to the next level is to become unethical. There are agents who don't treat their clients with the honor and integrity they deserve. They shade the truth to their clients and other agents. Some of these agents end up out of the business in a short period of time. Others manage to stay in business for years. These agents seem to be one step ahead of the ethics committee in their Board of Realtors or the state real estate agency. You will want to steer clear of this path. You could wake up one morning and be out of business.

Running Your Business As a Business

The last path is a business that generates regular income and is repeatable in clients and net profit. This path gives you control of your income and your time. It replicates a high net profit because you know your business. You understand the sales ratios that are in your business. You know the costs associated with your business and how to generate more revenue.

This path requires you to track your sales ratios and expenses. It requires that you prospect daily your past clients, sphere, expireds, FSBOs, or cold calls. The agents on this path create their income rather than react to the marketplace. They decide how much income they are going to earn monthly, quarterly, and yearly. They

"I'm the King of the World!"

I remember the exact time I realized I was on this path. It was the second week in January 1993. I was in the shower at 6:15 A.M. reviewing my day. I was going over my plan for the week and for the year. I remember thinking that I could make any amount of money I desired because I knew my sales ratios and how to create my business. It was one of the best feelings of accomplishment and satisfaction. You can have that same feeling of success of knowing where you are in your business and how you got there. There is truly no feeling in life that I can compare to it. The best analogy I can give you is in the movie *Titanic* when Leonardo DiCaprio was on the bow of the ship hanging over the rail shouting, "I'm the king of the world." That is the feeling you have when you realize how to create and replicate your business at will.

have the great feeling of satisfaction that they can repeat their performance at will.

Your Financial Investment at the Next Level

The financial investment that needs to be made to get to the next level in real estate is minimal compared to other businesses. If you compare the inventory of any retail operation that is selling a million dollars a year in products, our business investment as real estate agents is quite small. The initial investment for a retail operation is huge. And look at the investment in equipment that a dentist needs to earn $500,000 a year in gross revenue. A dentist has to have $500,000 to $1,000,000 in equipment just to open the doors of his practice.

As a real estate salesperson, you can earn what the doctor or dentist earns without this large overhead. Your overhead is merely your car, a cell phone, and a computer. You have the capacity to earn $100,000 your first year with equipment that you already own. How many businesses give you the same opportunity to earn such a high income with nothing down?

Your Knowledge Investment

The real investment we need to make to take our business to the next level is knowledge and skill. You need to be knowledgeable in all facets of real estate sales. Your investment in yourself will bring you the greatest dividends. Because you are new in the business you should take advantage of every educational opportunity available to you.

The more you know about the products and services that your company provides, the better you can take advantage of them for yourself and your clients.

Company Training

If your company provides training, then take every class that you can. The more you know about the products and services your company provides, the better you can take advantage of them for yourself and your clients. Most agents do not take full advantage of the services the broker is providing. In most cases you are paying for these services whether you use them or not. You are paying for them with your commission split. Make sure you are getting value for your investment in your company. Be familiar with all the tools it provides and use them.

Board Educational Opportunities

Most of the real estate boards or associations that you will need to join offer continuing education. They bring in expert speakers on technology, housing, investments, legal contracts, sales, time management, and many other subjects. Most of these training classes are free with your dues or you can attend for a very small fee.

Annual Conventions

Most state boards also have annual conventions. These state conventions give you the opportunity to exchange ideas with other agents. You can learn from some of the best agents in your area and across the state, and the state boards often bring in nationally known figures as keynote speakers. Many conventions have break-out sessions—smaller, more intimate training events. This gives you a choice of a number of different seminars to attend and learn the skills to mastery.

An advantage of being with a larger nationally based company is that they have national conventions as well. These meetings allow you to rub elbows with agents across North America and, in some cases, the world. These events are focused on the exchange of new ideas and techniques to expand your business. They also give you the opportunity to build a network of agents worldwide.

Independent Training Companies

There are also educational opportunities that are not company- or board-based. These are independent training companies for real estate professionals. These companies hold seminars, sell audiotapes and CDs, and publish literature on all facets of real estate.

Some trainers focus on technology, like Michel Russer, Steven Canale, or Mathew Ferrera. Their seminars are designed to help you master the steps to become skilled in technology to expand your income and ease of business operation. There are other speakers and companies that are more marketing based. They will teach you how

Networking

Developing a network of agents worldwide can increase your commission income and help generate more business for you now and in the future. Real estate agents often have the opportunity to earn income by referring clients. Many other professions are not allowed to do this. When your dentist refers you to a specialist like an orthodontist, he cannot be paid for the referral. As real estate agents, however, we have that opportunity. We can refer a buyer or seller to an agent in another state or even another country and receive 20 to 30 percent of the total commission paid. Other agents can refer clients who are moving to or from your area of business to you. This referral option in real estate sales can help you earn additional income by developing a database of other agents you know around the world. I know agents who make $100,000 a year or more just from inbound and outbound referrals. By attending national conventions you have the opportunity exchange your business cards and create strategic alliances with agents worldwide.

to expose yourself to the marketplace. Some will teach you how to build your individual brand. One of the best in the industry who can teach you the marketing angles of real estate is Mark McKee.

Other companies focus on sales skills. They teach you the skills of making the sale, keeping the client, and handling the objections in the selling process. An example of one of these training companies is my company, Real Estate Champions. This training category is often passed over by agents. We tend to gravitate to events that offer the magic answer to success. The sales skills category is, however, indispensable. A dentist without good hands is not much of a dentist. A salesperson without the right words and delivery is not much of a salesperson. Don't neglect this category of sales training. It may not be as sexy as marketing, but it's more important.

Training in Business Skills

Lastly, you need training in business skills to take your career to the next level: skills to understand what your expenses are, what it costs you to acquire a client, what your time is worth and how to gain control of it, and how to spend more time in high-dollar activities and less time in low-dollar activities. Some of this necessary training is available in CRS (Certified Residential Specialist) classes sponsored by the Association of Realtors. The only independent company that really provides this type of training is my company, Real Estate Champions. You have to learn how to create and control your business rather than just react to your business if your desire is to be a multimillion dollar producer. Remember that you will need the skills of a good CEO to master your business. Resolve to get the training you need to hit the mark.

> *You have to learn how to create and control your business rather than just react to your business if your desire is to be a multimillion dollar producer.*

Know Your Behavioral Style

Take your business to the next level by learning about your behavioral style. Your behavior style will determine how you should build your business and how you will interact with your clients and prospects. Knowing your behavioral style allows you to adapt when necessary. It gives you the ability to read people and communicate with them in their own behavioral pattern.

A handful of behavioral assessments are available. I would recommend taking a DISC assessment. Dr. William Marston, a clinical psychologist, created the DISC model. In 1928 Marston published *Emotions of Normal People*, which describes the theory of DISC. (He was also the inventor of the polygraph.) DISC measures observable behavior and emotions. It is a language of watching people. Great salespeople are good observers of people. They have the ability to read people and adapt to other people's behavior.

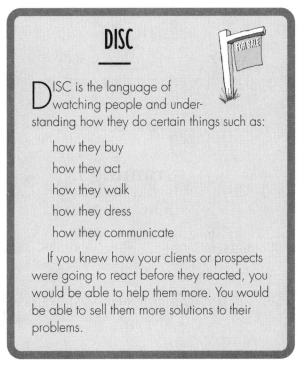

DISC

DISC is the language of watching people and understanding how they do certain things such as:

how they buy
how they act
how they walk
how they dress
how they communicate

If you knew how your clients or prospects were going to react before they reacted, you would be able to help them more. You would be able to sell them more solutions to their problems.

DISC is an acronym for the four major assessment groups: Dominance, Influencing, Steadiness, and Compliant.

Dominance: how you handle problems and challenges

Influencing: how you interact with other people

Steadiness: how you handle a steady pace and work environment

Compliant: how you respond to rules and procedures set by others

DISC Behavior Types

High "Dominants": Their natural tendency is to be active and aggressive at achieving a result. They are highly competitive and will face a problem with little or no fear. These people can cold call for business and it doesn't bother them. To them it's a means to the end. It's something they must do to reach the level of success they desire.

High "Influencers": They have a tendency to want a high degree of contact with people. They are outgoing, social, and verbally persuasive. These people need to build their business around their social relationships. They gain energy from people contacts.

High "Steadies": These are structured and predictable in their work environment. They prefer a secure situation. Their business has to be built through systems and structures that create results. They could create a mailing or advertising campaign. They could also create a prospecting process as long as it is not cold calling.

High "Compliants": They follow the rules set by others. They are also aware of the problems that arise when one doesn't follow the rules and procedures. These people struggle in real estate sales. It takes them a long time to make any money. They are so busy building the rules and procedures they make very few sales, but their paperwork is always impeccable.

We all have low or high scores in each area. These scores determine how we respond in a given situation or environment. All individuals have some of all of these factors in them. It is rare that we will exhibit only one behavioral factor. Four percent of the population exhibit behavior primarily from one factor. Fifty percent exhibit behavior combining two of the factors. Forty-six percent of the population exhibit behavior combining three of the factors.

By knowing your own DISC behavioral style, you can also recognize the styles of others. You will face these styles daily as prospects and clients. Some of these people are going to be quick to make a decision, like the Dominants and Influencers. Others are going to be slow, like the Steadies. Some are going to wait for the next millennium like the Compliants. You have to be able to recognize with whom you are dealing. This will enable you to take your sales career to the next level. The first step is to know yourself. Lao-tzu, the famous Chinese philosopher said, "He who knows others is learned. He who knows himself is wise."

Lao-tzu, the famous Chinese philosopher said, "He who knows others is learned. He who knows himself is wise."

If you need help with a DISC assessment, ask your broker. She may provide the assessment. Some of the large national companies are using DISC assessments. You could also contact our office at Real Estate Champions. We have an incredibly in-depth assessment that will provide you with the tools you need. You can reach us at 541-383-8833, or you can visit our Web site at www.realestatechampions.com. We have a number of assessments that will aid you in your career.

Solving Problems

A career in real estate sales can provide incredible income, incredible frustration, or both. The most exciting part of your new career is that you will receive what you put in. Your ability to learn and to continue to take calculated risks will eventually lead you to top honors in your company.

These chapters have covered what you need to know about relationships in your real estate career and the skills that will help you through your first year. Here are some frequently asked questions that we hear from new agents and a bit of final advice.

The most exciting part of your new career is that you will receive what you put in.

What Is the First Thing I Need to Do Once I Find a Broker to Work With?

Ask your broker for scripts, dialogues, and objection-handling techniques and then practice, practice, practice! Suppose your broker plans to teach you how to write contracts and listing agreements—what I call "Real Estate 101." Although this is very important, I would rather you begin by practicing your sales skills. We are all going to be successful in our real estate career based on our ability to sell. Therefore, it is vital for your success to study and practice the art of salesmanship.

Your ability to become a sales master will do more for your sales career than anything else you can do at this stage. Partner with another new agent and role-play your scripts and dialogues for the listing presentation, buyer interview, follow-up calls, and objection-handling every day. We play at the level we practice. If we rarely practice, as most agents do, our performance will reflect that fact.

What Is the Best Way for Me to Handle Problems?

Most solutions to the problems we experience in real estate are based on common sense. Fine-tune and use your common sense regularly. When something doesn't feel right there is usually a good reason. For example, when a buyer is evasive in his willingness to disclose the source of his down payment, it is quite often because he doesn't have the money and is hoping to raise it before closing. When buyers disappear every time you ask them to redeem their earnest money note for a check, this again means that they are short on funds or they are having second thoughts about their commitment to purchase this home.

Handle Problems Promptly

As real estate professionals, we are faced daily with these challenges. One element of being a professional is getting the situation handled right away. Too often we use the ostrich technique of problem solving—sticking your head in the sand hoping the problem will go away. The best technique for resolving a problem is to face it head on as soon as possible so you can either hold the transaction together or release the seller and buyer to go another direction. The longer the problem is left in limbo, the greater the agony when you finally release the deal.

Operate with Full Disclosure

Be sure to steer clear of all the gray areas in a real estate transaction. When you are working with clients or prospects and what they are telling you doesn't pass the litmus test, either confront them or disengage from them. Many people will prey on a new agent because that agent lacks the experience to see the challenges with clarity. For example, a buyer may ask you to not disclose to the lender that there is a second mortgage by another party, either the seller or another person.

It's easy to sidestep the truth when you need the money. We as professionals have an obligation because of the size of the investment and the emotions involved in buying or selling a home. But through it all you must avoid gray areas and keep to the straight and narrow path. The truth is seldom a superhighway. It's a narrow path with narrow gates at both ends. Therefore, we must operate with full disclosure at all times.

How Do I Get More Listings?

That question can be answered in a single word: prospect! If you are entering real estate sales, as most people do, without money to burn, start by prospecting. Learn the fundamentals of prospecting and be able to generate business from the regular application of that discipline. Set up a specific time and place to prospect and then do it. In the end, we are paid for action and for what we do. Become a person of action.

Your journey to become a "top gun" agent is just beginning. There will by many turns in the road ahead. If you get up each morning with a strong conviction that you are going to improve your skills and abilities each day, you will. If you make the commitment right now that you will prospect each day no matter what, you will win.

Sow New Seeds Every Day

Success is built by application of daily discipline. This law of success is illustrated by a biblical parable: A farmer went out to sow seed. Some of that seed fell on the path and was eaten by birds. Still other seed fell on rocky places; it sprang up, but without enough soil it soon withered. Other seed fell among the thorns and was eventually choked out. Some seed fell on good soil and it produced a crop 30, 60, or even 100 times what was sown.

Success is built by application of daily discipline.

The moral is: Keep sowing! Your job is to be like the farmer: Keep sowing new seeds every day. You will encounter all types of people when you sow—people on the path who aren't moving, people on rocky soil who are easily excited but won't take a deal to completion, and people who are thorny and negative all the time. The good part is you will find people who are fertile soil. These people will help build your real estate career. They will enable you to earn a high income and build the business we have described in this book. But remember that you must keep sowing.

Many agents expect every seed they sow to bring forth fruit. They get discouraged when each seed planted with a prospect doesn't germinate. However, don't worry so much about getting each seed to germinate; instead, just keep planting. Never stop planting new seeds. The farmer will always receive a crop if he plants long enough and consistently. Flood or drought may wipe out this year's crop, but eventually the crop will come in 30-, 60-, or even 100-fold.

So it will be with your real estate career. Resolve today to be great at sowing. Become a great prospector and your business and income will multiply. You have the gifts and ability to become great. The seeds of greatness have been sown inside of you by the Master Sower. You have begun the watering process with this book. You can become that "top gun" agent you desire to become.

> God's gift to you is more talent and ability than you could possibly use in a lifetime. Your gift to God is to develop as much of that talent and ability as you can in this lifetime.
>
> —Steve Bow (quoted in *The Science of Getting Rich* by Wallace Wattles)

Appendix I

State Realtor Associations

Alabama
  www.alabamarealtors.com/

Alaska
  www.realtorsofalaska.com/

Arizona
  www.aaronline.com/

Arkansas
  www.arkansasrealtors.com/

California
  www.car.org/

Colorado
  www.colorealtor.org/

Connecticut
  www.ctrealtor.com/

Delaware
  www.delawarerealtor.com/

District of Columbia
  www.gwcar.org/

Florida
  http://planetrealtor.com/
  default.asp

Georgia
  www.garealtor.com/

Hawaii
www.hawaiirealtors.com/

Idaho
www.idahorealtors.com/

Illinois
www.illinoisrealtor.org/

Indiana
http://indianarealtors.com/

Iowa
http://ia.living.net/

Kansas
www.kansasrealtor.com/

Kentucky
www.kar.com/

Louisiana
www.larealtors.org/members/
default.asp

Maine
www.mainerealtors.com/

Maryland
www.mdrealtor.org/

Massachusetts
http://ma.living.net/

Michigan
www.mirealtors.com/

Minnesota
http://mn.living.net/

Mississippi
http://ms.living.net/

Missouri
http://mo.living.net/

Montana
www.mtmar.com/public_html/
index.html

Nebraska
http://nebraskarealtors.com/

Nevada
www.nvrealtors.org/

New Hampshire
www.nhar.com/

New Jersey
www.njar.com/

New Mexico
http://nm.living.net/

New York
www.nysar.com/

North Carolina
www.realtor.org/

North Dakota
http://nd.living.net/

Ohio
www.ohiorealtors.com/

Oklahoma
www.oklahomaassociationofrealtors.com/

Oregon
http://or.realtorplace.com/

Pennsylvania
www.parealtor.org/

Rhode Island
www.riliving.com/

South Carolina
http://screaltors.com/

South Dakota
www.sdrealtor.org/

Tennessee
www.tarnet.com/

Texas
www.tar.org/

Utah
www.utahrealtors.com/

Vermont
www.vtrealtor.com/

Virginia
www.varealtor.com/index.asp

Washington
www.warealtor.com/

West Virginia
www.wvrealtors.com/

Wisconsin
www.wra.org/

Wyoming
http://wy.living.net/

Appendix II

Additional Reading

Clason, George. *The Richest Man in Babylon*. New American Library.

Clason describes in parable form the steps to achieve wealth in life.

Hill, Napoleon. *Think and Grow Rich*. Fawcett Books.

This is the original self-help book for successful professionals. As a young man, Napoleon Hill was commissioned by Andrew Carnegie to write the secret to success. Carnegie introduced Hill to all the movers and shakers of his era, like John D. Rockefeller, Henry Ford, and Thomas Edison. He distilled their secrets into this book.

Hopkins, Tom. *How to Master the Art of Listing and Selling Real Estate*. Prentice Hall.

This is a timeless classic on how to be successful in the real estate business. A must-read for any agent.

Rohn, Jim. *Seven Strategies for Wealth and Happiness*. Prima Publishing.

Jim shares how to achieve everything you want in life and how to craft the grand life you desire. Jim is America's foremost business philosopher.

Tracy, Brian. *Advanced Selling Strategies*. Fireside.

Brian shares the steps to being a master salesperson. You will learn the techniques to more effectively prospect, present, and close.

Tuccillo, John. *The Eight New Rules of Real Estate*. Real Estate Education Company.

This is a recent look at the changing face of real estate in the new millennium.

Audio Cassettes

Nightingale, Earl. *Lead the Field*. Nightingale-Conant Corporation.

Nightingale, Earl. *The Strangest Secret*. Nightingale-Conant Corporation.

Rohn, Jim. *The Art of Exceptional Living*. Simon & Schuster (Audio).

Tracy, Brian. *The Psychology of Selling*. Simon & Schuster (Audio).

Tracy, Brian. *The Psychology of Achievement*. Simon & Schuster (Audio).

Ziglar, Zig. *Goals*. Simon & Schuster (Audio).

Audio Books

Ziglar, Zig. *See You At The Top*. Pelican Publishing.

Zig teaches us to climb the mountain of success one step at a time. Zig is recognized as one of the greatest sales trainers and motivators in the world.

Relevant Magazines

Broker Agent

Broker Insider

Real Estate Champions Coaches
    Corner E-Zine

Real Estate Professional, The

Realtor Today

Selling Power

Web Sites

International Real Estate Digest:
    www.ired.com

National Association of Realtors:
    http://nar.realtor.com/

Online Real Estate
    Marketing Report:
    www.hometeam2000.com

Real Estate Champions:
    www.realestatechampions.com

Realty Times:
    www.realtytimes.com

Glossary

Abstract of title A complete summary of the public records of a piece of property that relates to the title. An attorney or title company reviews this and determines the defects in the title before the property transfer.

Agreement of sales A contract in which a seller agrees to sell and a buyer agrees to buy under specific terms and conditions. These terms and conditions are clearly spelled out in writing. Also known as purchase agreement, sales agreement, contract of purchase, or earnest money agreement.

Appraisal An estimate of value of real property on a given date. A mortgage company usually requires one before a loan is granted.

Closing costs The expense in addition to the sale price that buyers and sellers incur to complete the transfer of ownership from the seller to the buyer.

Buyer's Expenses:

Recording fee for deed and mortgage

Escrow fees

Attorney fees

Mortgage fees

Points

Document prep fee

Origination fees

Appraisal

Home inspection

Title insurance

Seller's Expenses:

Abstract of title

Real estate commission

Escrow fees

Attorney fees

Recording of the deed

Release of deed of trust

Closing day The day when transfer of title is concluded. The buyer and seller sign the final papers and recording of the deed takes place at the county. All final documents are signed, that is, the deed of trust.

Cloud on the title An encumbrance that negatively affects the marketability of the title. This cloud needs to be removed before transfer can take place.

Commission What is paid to the real estate broker by the seller for the completion of the sale between the buyer and the seller.

Cooperative broker A real estate broker who brings an offer or a sales agreement to the listing broker on behalf of a buyer.

Deed The legal instrument used to transfer ownership of a property from the current owner to the buyer. There are two parties in a deed, grantor and grantee.

Deed of trust A security instrument used in many areas by a mortgage company to secure its position on real property. This deed of trust allows the trustee to sell the property at a public sale if there is a default by the purchasers.

Default Failure by the purchaser to make mortgage payments as agreed to based on the terms agreed upon.

Down payment The amount of money to be paid by the purchaser at the time of closing that goes toward the purchase price of real property. This down payment, plus closing costs, plus mortgage are the costs needed to close a transaction.

Earnest money The deposit money given to the seller by the buyer upon initial offer of the agreement of sale. If all parties agree to the agreement of sale, the earnest money becomes part of the down payment.

Encumbrance A legal interest in real property that affects clear title and can diminish the value of the property. Encumbrances can be easement rights, mortgages, liens, unpaid taxes, zoning ordinances, conditions, covenants, and restrictions of a subdivision.

Equity The encumbrance value of a property owner's real property. Usually computed by subtracting the mortgage balance and encumbrances and fees for selling from the property's fair market value.

Escrow An independent third party that holds the funds and prepares the documents in a real estate transaction. This party cannot act without written instructions from both parties (the buyer and seller).

Expireds Properties that have been listed by a real estate broker and remain unsold. The exclusive right-to-sell listing contract between the broker and seller has reached its term and is no longer in force.

Foreclosure The enforcement of payment of the secured debt by a deed of trust or mortgage holder. Often enforced by selling mortgaged property at a sheriff's sale.

FSBOs (For Sale By Owners) People who are trying to sell their home on their own without the aid of a real estate broker.

General warranty deed or statutory warranty deed Conveys all interests of the grantor of title of property to the grantee. It also warrants the property is clear of all encumbrances except what goes with the property, for example, zoning ordinances, and CC & Rs. This also allows the grantee to hold the grantor liable if encumbrances appear later.

Grantee The buyer on the deed.

Grantor The seller on the deed.

Hazard insurance Property insurance against fire required by most mortgage companies before closing.

Lien A claim on a property by another who is owed money. This is a security instrument. A lien could include unpaid property taxes, judgments, homeowners' dues, or construction or contractor bills that are unpaid.

Marketable title A title to the property that is free and clear of all liens and encumbrances that don't go with the property permanently. It allows the seller to sell and the buyer to buy.

Mortgage A lien against real property given by the buyer to the lender. The mortgage is security against the money borrowed by the buyer.

Mortgage commitment A document from a lending institution that guarantees that it will provide a certain amount of funds for the buyer to use to purchase real property.

Mortgagee The lender in a mortgage agreement.

Mortgagor The borrower in a mortgage agreement.

Points Often called discount points. A point is paid to lower interest rates. It is pre-paid interest in advance at the time of closing. A single point is one percent of the amount of the mortgage loan.

Quitclaim deed A deed that transfers the interest one has in a piece of real property. There is no warranty element of a quitclaim deed. The buyer assumes all the risk by accepting a quitclaim deed.

Real estate agency The state's governing body that controls and regulates the activities of real estate brokers and agents, and, in many states, title and escrow companies as well.

Real estate agent Helps people buy and sell homes, office buildings, industrial property, and corporation farmland and handles property management and land development. Licensing is required and can vary across the nation, but all states require prospective salespeople to pass a written exam.

Real estate broker With more experience and upon passing of an additional exam, the next step beyond being a real estate agent. Brokers can own their own businesses and employ other real estate agents.

Survey A map or plat of the dimensions of the land based on its relationship to the surrounding parcels, created by a licensed surveyor. Can often be required by a lender to assure them of the value of property and that buildings are sited on the right parcel.

Title Ownership interest one has in real property; may also refer to document by which ownership interest is established.

Title insurance Protects the buyer and lender against a loss against their interest if later legal defects or clouds are found on the title.

Title search A check of the title records by either an attorney or a title company at the courthouse. This ensures that no unforeseen encumbrances or liens appear later that would adversely affect the value of the property.

Index

About the Author _____

Dirk Zeller started his real estate career in 1990. Working for a major, national real estate company, he quickly distanced himself from the crowd by becoming a top ten producer in units sold and commission earned in a four state, 1400 agent region. Dirk has been described by industry experts as "the realtor who created the ideal real estate business" because of his ability to sell 150 homes annually while working a Monday through Thursday workweek and taking Friday, Saturday, and Sunday off to be with his family.

Dirk is a highly accomplished author with over 200 different articles published on real estate sales and life success. His articles have appeared in such national publications as *The Real Estate Professional, Broker Agent Magazine, Broker Insider, Realty Times* and *International Real Estate Digest*, as well as countless regional, state, and local publications.

He is also one of the most sought after professional speakers in the real estate industry, addressing such topics as sales strategies, time management, motivation, and life balance. Dirk has shared the stage with such notable speakers as Zig Ziglar.

Dirk is the CEO and head coach of Real Estate Champions, which provides business consulting, coaching, and development training for real estate companies, managers, and agents worldwide. He and his wife, Joan, live in Bend, Oregon.

Real Estate Champions

TAPE SERIES

Real Estate Champions Objection Handling **Tape Series & Workbook:** The most complete guide to handling the objections that come up in the sales process. We teach you the process of mental mastery. How to prepare for objections from buyers and sellers. The tape series also teaches you three to four techniques for all the objections in selling real estate. …$295.00

The Five Steps To Having Your Best Year Ever **Tape Series:** This tremendous tape series helps you put the pieces in place to dramatically increase your production. Learn to power plan, to be effective not just efficient. Learn to apply the power of sales ratios to explode your business to the next level. ……………………………………………………………………………$59.00

Survivor Sales Training **Tape Series & Workbook:** This tape series covers Sales Success Skills, Defining Your Job Description, Characteristics of Sales Champions, Price Reductions, Objection Handling, Overcoming Call Reluctance, and Closing Techniques. Interview with two of our clients that increased production over 10 million in one year. It's a great, value-packed series. ………$295.00

The Champions Summit **Tape Series & Workbook:** This is a "live" taping of the Champions Summit event. The best agents across North America gathered at this event to learn how to mind read their customer and adapt their communication to increase sales, how to read and understand the different behavior styles, how to conduct a values-based interview with a prospect or client, the process of Stewardship Selling™, and how to create rock-solid client commitment from everyone they meet. These agents also learned how to motivate, train, and build their teams. They learned from two of the top agents in the country, Julie Boyd-Elrod and John Gualtieri, how these two agents doubled their production in less than one year. ……………………$395.00

MANUALS

Success Building System **Manual:** This manual has the steps we used to efficiently take you from lead generation to the listing appointment, from the listing taken to the sale, then from the sale of the property to the close. Includes checklists for efficiency; letters of correspondence; scripts for contact with clients and prospects; and information on hiring, training, and coaching staff. This tool will enable you to reduce your time working "in" your business, so you can spend more time in growing your business. ……………………………………………………………………………………………$99.00

SPECIAL BOOK PRICING!	RETAIL	SPECIAL BOOK PRICING
Power Package #1—The whole package	$1,140.00	$575.00
Real Estate Champions Objection Handling Tape Series • *The Five Steps To Having Your Best Year Ever* Tape Series • *Survivor Sales Training* Tape Series • *The Champions Summit* Tape Series • *Success Building System* Manual		
Power Package #2—Sales Skills	$985.00	$475.00
Real Estate Champions Objection Handling Tape Series • *Survivor Sales Training* Tape Series • *The Champions Summit* Tape Series		
Power Package #3—Team Building	$553.00	$375.00
The Champions Summit Tape Series • *Success Building System* Manual • *The Five Steps To Having Your Best Year Ever* Tape Series		
Power Package #4—Jumpstart	$453.00	$275.00
Survivor Sales Training Tape Series • *Success Building System* Manual • *The Five Steps To Having Your Best Year Ever* Tape Series		

To order any of our products, please feel free to call our office at **1-877-RECHMPN** or visit our website at **www.realestatechampions.com.**

Every Rental Property Manager's Complete Handbook

Although many property managers lose more money each year on maintenance or long vacancies than they make in profit, with the right management system and some business savvy, you can rent out a house or condominium and still have enough time to enjoy your growing profits—or purchase more properties! Greg Perry shows you how! Inside, you'll learn valuable money-saving tips, such as how to:

- **Market your property to attract droves of prospective tenants**
- **Keep good tenants happy and get rid of bad tenants**
- **Use the Internet to market your rentals**
- **Choose the right insurance and prepare your taxes**
- **And much, much more!**

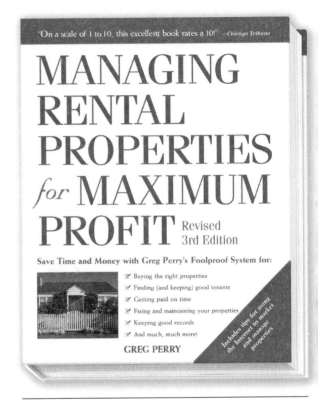

ISBN 0-7615-2531-9 / Paper over board
336 pages / U.S. $24.95 / Can. $37.95

Organize Your Whole Company for Sales Success

In today's highly technical, information-driven business environment, every employee in your company can now be an important player on your sales team. That means every employee must know how to sell well, sales professionals must understand how to leverage the expertise of other players, and team leaders—executive and managers—must know how to organize the team to maximize performance.

In *Selling Is a Team Sport,* expert sales consultant Eric Baron reveals how to create, train, and play on a company-wide selling team. His proven problem-solving approach to selling will have all members of your company ready to respond to your customers' needs and maximize your sales performance.

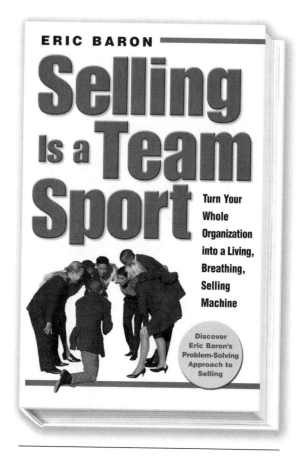

ISBN 0-7615-2530-0 / Hardcover
320 pages / U.S. $24.95 / Can. $37.95

For Americans on the Move—
the ULTIMATE Relocating Guides